Finding a Public Voice:

Using Barbara Fister as a Case Study

Edited by
Danielle Theiss and Diane Kovacs

D1547880

Association of College and Research Libraries
A division of the American Library Association
Chicago 2013

The paper used in this publication meets the minimum requirements of American National Standard for Information Sciences–Permanence of Paper for Printed Library Materials, ANSI Z39.48-1992. ∞

Library of Congress Cataloging-in-Publication Data

Finding a public voice : using Barbara Fister as a case study / edited by Danielle Theiss and Diane Kovacs.
    pages cm
  Includes bibliographical references and index.
  ISBN 978-0-8389-8652-3 (pbk. : alk. paper) 1. Academic librarians--United States. 2. Academic libraries--Relations with faculty and curriculum--United States 3. Fister, Barbara--Career in library science. 4. Libraries and colleges--United States. 5. Communication in library science--United States. 6. Library orientation for college students--United States. I. Theiss, Danielle. II. Kovacs, Diane K. (Diane Kaye), 1962-
  Z682.4.C63F56 2013
  027.70973--dc23
                                2013020153

Acknowledgements

Thank you to Melanie Church who read through the edited chapters and provided feedback and to library student assistants Brian Golka, Caitlyn Tilden and Jeremiah Laurent for checking citations. Thanks also to Rockhurst University and Laurie Hathman, Director of Greenlease Library, for supporting this endeavor.

~Danielle Theiss

Thank you to Danielle Theiss who did most of the real work for this book. ;)

~Diane Kovacs

Table of Contents

A Haiku

Cheryl LaGuardia
Research Librarian, Widener Library, Harvard University

Dear Barbara Fister,
you make me so proud to be
a librarian.

Brave Barbara Fister

Cheryl LaGuardia
(in homage to Barbara and John Greenleaf Whittier)

Up from the stacks all rich with lore,
clear in the cool library morn,
the clustered spires of academe stand
fed by knowledge from Libraryland.

Round about them students sleep,
young brains resting in slumber deep.
Their learning will resume as soon
as they arise, at nearly noon.

The students' heads were filled with history,
Bio 101, and other mysteries.
They loved to learn, they loved their classes,
'til just a few words turned their dreams to ashes.

On that pleasant day in the early fall
when their professors sounded the frightening call—
"A research paper's required," they said,
filling the students' hearts with dread.

"You'll need forty sources from scholarly media,
and those forty sources cannot come from *Wikipedia*."
The students' jaws flapped in the wind—
by that last injunction, their hopes were thinned.

Forty scholarly sources? How was that possible?
Not use *Wikipedia*? The prospects were horrible.
Their grades depended on sound research,
but poor research skills left them deep in the lurch.

Up rose good Barbara Fister then,
armed with her MLIS and pen;
bravest of all in Knowledge town,
she took on a task others might have turned down.

She didn't flinch, she didn't falter,
She simply made a simple offer.
In her office window the notice she set,
to show that her heart was undaunted yet.

"To any student wanting to learn
how information works, or how to turn
away from the iffy sources, and towards the scholarly,
then come right in, and if you'll follow me

"I'll show you the way to search, and to filter,
pose interesting questions—how to un-bewilder
the research process in all its glory—
citation's yet another story

"with which I can help you, and what is more,
you'll find library research is really no chore!
I'll show you to quote and properly phrase
so you'll never, ever plagiarize."

"I've much that can help you," she merrily said,
"let's start with a database or two," she bade.
"*Google Scholar* and *JSTOR* are full of good lore
but I'd like you to know that there's just so much more."

And so, as a group, they went on a search journey,
'mongst paper and digits, they found themselves turning
to a multitude of sources, way beyond only Google,
some of them online, some of them tactile.

"Library databases are good," her cohort she coached,
"Open Access journals, too, can often be broached.
The key is to search, discover, and filter,
And then leave a trail for others to consider."

"A bibliography should be that trail," she noted,
"and that's one reason why you cite all whom you've quoted.
So others can follow your argument to
the point where you've synthesized something quite new."

As she spoke, students listened, and thought, and tried out
the sources she'd showed them, assessing throughout
the source of the source, the authority of the writer,
and if the info. came from an unbiased provider.

They began thinking critically, aware that at times
an author was trying to mess with their minds.
They must chew on ideas, see different perspectives—
research was the way to determine objectives.

And when an author hasn't done all the research they aught
we must digest what they say with a grain of salt.
"Consider the source," means a lot in the academy;
so too, should it mean much in life for you (and me).

This realization came not as an eye-blinding flash,
but it gradually built, became part of a cache
of knowledge about how to find and consider
most any idea, belief, or opinion.

And Barbara, game teacher, and writer, and coach
encouraged the students to question and broach
the difficult questions, the ones that could dig out
concepts whose validity one really should doubt.

In all of her teaching, her writing, her talks
she aims for the truth, and shakes out the faux.
She's thoroughly grounded, in knowledge and skills,
decries "shiny new things," spits out vendor's sour pills.

She advocates MOOCs, flipped classrooms, open source—
dislikes "Faustian library bargains" and exploitative commerce.
The "enclosure of knowledge" is one grave concern,
as is eBook overpricing, a recent publishing upturn.

In a quote that is likely to increase her fame
she describes "book distribution as a brutal mashup of Upton Sinclair's
The Jungle and Suzanne Collins's *The Hunger Games*."
One can see Barbara Fisters' work is not o'er,
for the library raiders ride on their raids more and more.

All honor to her! and let us here cheer
for her work, for her teaching, her writing, and more.
Let this book, in its way, hereby so proclaim
our respect and regard for Barbara's name.

Peace, order, and beauty should rightly come
to this wonderful symbol of librarydom;
and ever the stars up above should look down
on this bright star among us in Library town!

Preface

Steven J. Bell

Associate University Librarian, Research & Instructional Services, Paley Library, Temple University

When ACRLog, the Association of College and Research Libraries' commentary blog, was in the early stages of implementation, I was asked to develop the concept for this new forum for sharing ideas and opinions about the issues of day of concern to academic librarians. A number of the blogs at that time were authored by individual academic librarians, but to truly reflect the diverse interests of ACRL and its members it seemed that a group approach might work best. So I set out to assemble a team of the best academic librarian thinkers and writers I could find.

As I considered which academic librarians to invite as participants in this new venture, the first person that came to my mind was Barbara Fister. I didn't know Barbara. I had never met her, and I didn't need to. All I needed to know was that she had definite opinions on any number of issues, was willing to take on those topics for which there are no easy answers and was a great writer who could passionately argue for a cause and articulate her thoughts with great clarity and just the right amount of sarcasm. All are highly desirable qualities of a great blogger.

I knew these things because I followed the COLLIB-L discussion list for academic librarians. In those days Barbara was a frequent commenter, and developed a reputation for both introducing important issues and jumping in to almost any debate. Where her posts to the list shined most was when the discussion turned to the scholarly communications issues, publishing industry inequities and almost any issue that concerned the education of our students. When Barbara was asked to blog for ACRLog she agreed right away, and it worked out exceedingly well.

Even if Barbara never blogged for ACRLog, given her talent she was certainly destined for bigger things and more demands on her time. While many academic librarians are good at one form of communication, perhaps scholarly publication, blogging, tweeting or public presentation, Barbara is the Renaissance person of academic librarianship. She has the unique ability to cross between all forms of publishing, be it blogging, academic scholarship, essays, and of course her work as an author of multiple mystery books. It's no wonder that she is in heavy demand for all types of writing and presenting.

I know she probably won't like the comparison, but I'm going to go ahead and suggest that Barbara is like the Steve Jobs of librarianship. Like Jobs, she's brilliant and sees things no one else does by smartly connecting the dots. She can be brash and isn't afraid to tell you what she thinks—especially when it comes to publishers or vendors of library services and products. When Agent Fister is on the case these folks had better watch out. Barbara knows that to transform the culture of librarianship, she must be completely open, authentic and honest—to the point of expressing anger, frustration, joy and hope on any of the many issues she takes on in her columns and blog posts. Like Jobs, it is the transparency and honesty that her fans admire and love most about Barbara. She tells it like it is. It's also in the way she tells it. Few librarians in any segment of the professional share Barbara's knack for finding just the right words to describe any situation—and she often cracks us up doing it.

Perhaps the ultimate test of an academic librarian's contributions to the profession is the impact that his or her work has beyond the boundaries of librarianship. That is, to what extent did he or she influence the thinking of faculty, administrators and even students? As you read the essays of non-librarian academics, on almost any occasion when their attention turns to student research, scholarly communications or publishing, it's no surprise there are references to Barbara's writings. At her own institution we know that Barbara's leadership inspires colleagues and students to think differently about the library and their own research endeavors.

Barbara's influence on the thinking of her library colleagues clearly shines through in this collection of essays. Perhaps influence is too weak a word to describe how she inspires us, at least that's the impression I get when I read Cheryl LaGuardia's poetic tribute to Barbara. What better way to kick off this book than an ode to "Brave Barbara Fister." The first section of this book is dedicated to change. As a book that reflects on a career devoted to challenging academic librarians to change themselves and their institutions—and developing the voice to do it—perhaps it is fitting then to begin with a chapter that studies the ever changing career paths of academic librarians. In their chapter titled "Academic Librarianship and Career Adaptability" Tara Baillargeon and Aaron Carlstrom offer an essay on the four attributes needed for a good career. In many of her writings Barbara has reflected on change during the course of her career, and Baillargeon and Carlstrom are inspired by that to share their insights on how to successfully adapt to the change we will all experience as academic librarians. In her essays Barbara speaks to the importance of self-reflection to continually improve the library's institutional value and in their chapter "Missouri Universities, Librarians, and Accreditation: A Survey of Librarians' Involvement in the Self-study Processes", Laurie Hathman and Danielle Theiss surveyed Missouri librarians about their roles in recent accreditation and self-study processes at their institutions. They discovered that when academic librarians participate in accreditation related activities it increases awareness of and helps to demonstrate the library's value across the institution.

With a reputation as an educator who advocates for rethinking how we help students learn and what makes for the best assignments to develop research skills, Barbara has inspired many academic librarians to do likewise. Thus the next section of essays dwell on student learning and research.

Authors Kacy Lundstrom and Erin Davis "Clearing Up Mixed Messages in Library Instruction" share what has worked well for them at their institution as they've focused on how they communicate with faculty, students and library colleagues to deliver library instruction that focuses on building critical thinking skills. Fister's fellow Library Society of the World members, Iris Jastram and Steve Lawson, continue the appreciation of Barbara's wit and wisdom for librarian-educators with their chapter titled "Swimming in the Matrix: A Dialogue on Teaching Undergraduate Research." Making use of a conversation approach, they seek to achieve a deeper understanding of their goals as instruction librarians. In sharing both their frustrations about and aspirations for library instruction, Jastram and Lawson use a method well known to Barbara's readers to develop a better appreciation of how academic librarians can truly integrate themselves into the undergraduate learning process.

By focusing just on theological education in his chapter "Nurturing Virtuous Readers," M. Patrick Graham explores the territory where Barbara encourages learning through reading. Graham brings a unique focus by helping us to understand how applying the four key virtues to our instruction can help us prepare our students for a world of constant distraction. Concluding the section on instruction and learning is a contribution from Joanne Hélouvry titled "Student-centered Library use." We know from Barbara's writings that she believes that the library is a sacred space, and that even the book stacks are a place of discovery and learning. Hélouvry's contribution demonstrates the use of ethnographic methods to better understand which students use the library and how they use it. After a thorough review of what we have learned about the library as place and what it tells us about the value the library brings to its campus, she reminds the reader that it was Barbara Fister who said "Our libraries are places that learners lay claim to as a base camp, cartographers beginning an adventure into the unknown. We only need to welcome them inside so they can find a table and a window and make it their own." In the next chapter, "Building Bridges from the Ivory Tower," Anne Marie Deitering picks up on Barbara's mission to help her students connect the scholarly ideas they discover in the classroom with what matters in the real world. Deitering explores this idea, and reinforces the important role academic librarians can play in helping their students connect academic research to the challenges they will confront in the real world.

The final section of the book covers a topic that is often the target of Barbara Fister's ire: the publishers. It is the e-book and publisher policies for libraries in particular upon which Barbara is most apt to unleash her fury. That's where Rebecca Hamlett contributes with her chapter "E-Books: the Future of Our Readership?" She shares insights into the process her college library is going through to transition from a print to electronic collection, and e-books, along with reader technology, are a key component of the strategy. Mistakes were made, but the staff learned how to adapt and now are able to provide increased access to digital content. P.F. Anderson adds the final chapter to this section with a piece titled "The Burning Barn: Transparency and Privacy in e-Science and e-Health." Anderson chooses a topic near and dear to Barbara's heart, privacy and openness. In this essay he connects the important work of academic librarians to keep the researcher's actual research private, but to advocate for making it as openly accessible as possible.

Too often academic librarians lament that their work goes unrecognized and unappreciated on campus and within the larger scope of librarianship and even of higher education. Barbara Fister defies such conventions. That is why she deserves such high recognition, so that others will both be inspired by her contributions and passion, and take lessons from her successful career about what it means to be a courageous academic librarian leader and a voice of the community. I certainly have.

Speaking For Myself

Barbara Fister
Professor, Folke Bernadotte Memorial Library, Gustavus Adolphus College

So, here's a confession: I'm not brave. I have plenty of opinions, it's true, and I live in an era when expressing them publicly is incredibly easy. I have smart friends who know a lot more than I do about many things and (given that many of them are librarians and all of them are generous) they are quick to share their knowledge, and that makes it even easier to stay on top of things, encounter interesting news, and form opinions about whatever is going on.

But let's put this in perspective: I'm not as brave as young people who are the first in their family to go to college and who risk not only failure, but alienation from their family and friends because they're stepping over a border into an unfamiliar world, or people who stand on windy corners waiting for a bus to take them to their second minimum-wage job, or people who care for chronically sick children or aging parents, or even that adjunct faculty member who just set up an instruction session with a librarian before confessing she won't be there. Annoying though that may be, it could be that she's piecing together teaching gigs at three universities and spends every evening marking papers, and she's trying to get everything organized as she travels to a conference she can't afford so that if she's really, really on her game and lucky to boot, she might land a job with benefits and a salary that will bring her income above the poverty line. These are people who have enough courage to keep going without much encouragement in the hope that what they do might make things better or simply because they want to do what's right even if they have few options.

That's brave. Me, I'm lucky.

I was lucky to be born in an era when people thought it made sense for everyone to have an education, including college if they wanted it. My elementary education was actually at a Catholic school, where there were some formidable English teachers behind those wimples, but when it came time to go to college I was able to go to a good public university without ever having to even think of borrowing money. I could get by with minimum wage jobs in campus libraries and the art museum, and still had plenty of time to stop by my professors' offices to chat about whatever was on my mind. Maybe they were as frantically busy as faculty are today, but if so, it didn't show. They had cartoons and newspaper clippings taped to their doors, which were open most of the time, and we talked about everything under the sun.

I was lucky enough to start my adult life after college with no pressing worries, casually assuming I'd find work that would pay the rent, even with a major as useless as Russian literature. Older relatives used to frown with concern when they heard what I was studying and say "I guess you'll be a translator at the UN, then," because they couldn't think of anything else it was good for. I'd have to confess my Russian was terrible; the only thing I was any good at was reading big, fat novels and writing papers. But that, at the time, was a good place to start.

I entered grad school, but quickly realized that I really wanted to be an eternal undergraduate, not a specialist mining a narrow seam of scholarship, competing for tenured positions, and writing obscure monographs, so I wandered over to the library school to see if they would have me. No worries, the dean said. I could start taking courses in the spring.

My Russian graduate advisor who tried to talk me out of it told me "working in a library isn't like *working* in a library" as he poured me a glass of sherry. (I am not making this up—he kept a decanter of sherry handy for when he needed to dissuade a grad student from leaving the program.)

He thought that only the kind of research scholars like him did would be intellectually satisfying. But I found out he was wrong. Librarianship is challenging, creative, and rewarding work. Better yet, I soon discovered I could continue my undergraduate exploration of just about anything that catches my eye.

And, though I wasn't expecting it, there was another benefit to working in libraries. If I recall correctly, there were approximately four tenure-track jobs open in Russian Studies in the entire country the semester I tried it out. No wonder each of the graduate students was trying hard to be the best. It was as if there was a high stakes competition going on in every conversation, and whoever could quote the most French theorists won . But I wanted to work with people who could kick ideas around without always trying to score a goal. Librarians, I found out, are good at working with one another. Helping people out is what we do. Showing off, not so much.

At times, this reluctance to stand out can make it harder to do what we do. As T. Scott Plutchak has pointed out, we tend to act as if there are no people involved in making things happen at the library. We attribute new programs, resources, ideas, and projects to the building we work in. The library did it. In reality people did, people so invested in helping others that they have a tendency to erase themselves and make it all seem automatic, a frictionless mechanical platform for the care and feeding of other peoples' ideas, no human effort or thought involved.[1]

Why do we do that? Why aren't we bubbling over with excitement about our discipline? Librarians have the best job on earth! And there's so much more to do.

I've been lucky to have wandered haphazardly into a profession that has been going through amazing changes and is incapable of being dull. Who wouldn't love being a librarian these days? I know that students embarking on an MLS are heartily tired of being asked "why ever would you go into a profession that's going extinct?" but we know that's nonsense. These unenlightened would-be advisors see an edge to fall over, because to them the world extends only to the point where they can't see further. We want to see what's just over the horizon, because we know there's more, lots more, than what we can see from here. In some ways, that's the essence of our field.

Every morning is a brave new world full of challenges and new things to explore. Every semester brings a new crop of students who have so much to learn. Every time I take two minutes to look at my Twitter stream I find fifteen more things I want to read and learn about. But underlying all the bubbling change, which can at times be a little overwhelming, is a foundation of solid values, big generous values that support everything we do and seem to have a magnetic field embedded in them that gives us cardinal points to refer to when we're not sure which direction to go in.

When I started working at my first full-time library job, which happens to be the same one I'm in now (except like Hereclitus's stream, I walk into a different library every day), I was the second librarian at that college to have "bibliographic instruction" in my position title. I followed on the heels of an energetic librarian who had left me a filing cabinet brimming with class handouts and floppy disks full of Wordstar documents for the class material she'd developed. She had blazed quite a trail, conducting a needs assessment, establishing relationships with faculty, teaching a formidable number of library sessions. She moved on to other things, and I arrived just as the card catalog was being supplanted by an online catalog. My first task, I was told, would be instructing people how to use it. As it happened, it wasn't a big deal; people figured it out pretty quickly, though every now and then during those first years it went down. One member of the English department who taught courses on the beat poets used to take the personal offense whenever the terminals became unresponsive and would take poetic license to curse at that blinking cursor, walking away from the terminal leaving a screen full of a four-letter words as a kind of blank verse.

But though I was only the second librarian charged with instruction, I came to realize a learning focus for the library was nothing new. I stumbled across a document in the files written by a visionary library director who described our library as a teaching library back in the 1950s, who wrote in a 1965 planning document for the building I work in today, that the focus would be "more on *student* learning and less on *faculty* teaching." The library was being designed to bring students and ideas together in conversation, and it's working pretty well.

Since I was the only librarian involved in teaching (except at the reference desk, where everyone took a turn), I felt a little lonely. We had a very traditional organization, but being small, each of us had our area of specialty. We could go off to conferences once a year to meet fellow practitioners and read journal articles in the meantime. I could talk about teaching with faculty in other departments, and those involved in our writing across the curriculum program seemed to be thinking about the same issues that consumed me. But it wasn't enough. I had too much to learn.

It was an extraordinary thing when I signed on to BI-L, started by Martin Raish in 1990, which I think of as the year I got connected. It was amazing to sit at my desk in a small library in a small town in Minnesota and be in touch with hundreds of people interested in the same things I was, with ideas I could use, who were working out what librarians should do to support meaningful student learning in libraries all over the place. It was magic. And it was a place made up of nothing but people's voices, engaged in a conversation that never ended. Some of those conversations, in fact, were cyclical. At least once a year it seemed we had to hash out whether it was better to work our teaching into existing courses or whether we should be developing our own. Though we never came to agreement, we had a good time thrashing out the pros and cons of each approach. In 2002, the list was adopted by ALA and became ILI-L, which as I write has over 5,000 members. That's a lot of company, and a lot of conversations over a couple of decades.

I was trying out my voice, as well, with traditional publications. The first article I sent out to a journal disappeared into a black hole. After months of anxious waiting I wrote to see what had happened to it, and I got my first rejection letter of many. It was humbling, even humiliating, but I read through the manuscript again and thought to myself "this is *good.*" So I poked around and found another possible home for it and it was accepted—and then turned up on the LIRT list of the twenty best instruction articles of the year.

This is the kind of story I like to share with students: if you believe in what you have to say, don't give up too easily. I also share the time I got a reasoned rejection and thought "they're right. There's really not much substance, here" and chalked it up to experience. And the times I got conflicting reviews, including ones with bulleted lists of everything that was fatally wrong with my research, and how, after gritting my teeth and mumbling things under my breath, addressing those points made my work stronger.

The second article I wrote came out of a connection I'd forged with the director of our writing program who was hired the same year I was, which led me to explore some of the literature in her field. I was impressed by some of Janet Emig's work on the writing process and thought I could make a totally original contribution to the field. Tenure, here I come! While working on a small grant application to fund the work, I got up to stretch and strolled out of the office to check my mailbox, where I found a journal routed to me. As soon as I opened it, I saw that someone else had the very same idea and had gotten there first, this annoying woman named Carol Kulthau, who had done her dissertation under—I could hardly believe my eyes—Janet Emig. I was crushed, but only for a few minutes. I decided it just went to show that I was on to a good thing. Other people were interested in this subject! So I got back to work on the grant proposal and did the research and had a great time interviewing students about their experiences.

Another chance encounter led to the chance to publish my first book. When I attended a talk at my first ACRL conference given by a man who grew completely flustered when he couldn't get his microphone to work, I could feel people all around me tuning him out. I heard one neighbor mutter "he's not a teacher." But I disagreed; while he wasn't a great performer, he had great ideas for the classroom. I took my courage in both hands and went up to him after the talk and said "that was fascinating. Do you have time to go get a cup of coffee?" It turned out he was grateful for the company, feeling deflated by the audience response. We corresponded for a while, and when we met at another conference, he asked what I was working on. I'd heard an English professor say he had trouble finding literature by third world women for his syllabus, and I thought there was a need for a handbook on that topic. He put me touch with an editor at Greenwood, who asked for a proposal and quickly signed off on it, just in time for my tenure application.

See, I told you I was lucky. And I even got to read a lot of lovely fat books again.

There's nothing magical about finding a public voice. We each come to our work with a voice of our own. It just needs to be coaxed out with crumbs of curiosity and given regular exercise in conversations on campus, emails with friends, on Twitter or Facebook or on those venerable discussion lists. There are so many intriguing conversations going on around us, so many questions to ask, so many problems to solve.

I fell into writing fiction for reasons not so different than my professional writing. In the mid-1990s, we totally reorganized the way we work together in my library. It was a time full of creativity, but also of conflict, and it wasn't always easy to see the bigger picture. I realized one day that I was getting sour on life in the library, spending too much of my energy feeling angry and defeated. One evening, leaving work after meetings full of frustration, I thought to myself "I could *just kill*…" and stopped myself. That wasn't me. I am not homicidal. I was taking small matters far too seriously and needed to find some balance in my life. If I was going to kill anybody, I'd do it in my spare time, legally, on paper.

I had grown up surrounded by newspapers and books. My father was a journalist who, by the time I came along, was teaching journalism; my mother was a self-educated reader who always had a stack of mysteries nearby, most of them British. I got an education in Golden Age mysteries by reading her copies of Dorothy L. Sayers, Josephine Tey, Ngaio Marsh, and Margery Allingham. After getting intrigued by a homicidal maniac named Raskolnikov and following him into the darker realms of Dostoevsky and his countrymen, I returned to reading mysteries during what could be characterized as a new golden age. Though often thought of as escapist fiction, I found that it was possible with contemporary mysteries to do that magic trick described by Cyril Connolly[2] of giving us an escape not from but *into* life. The best crime fiction writers, I learned when I rediscovered mysteries, were writing about social issues in terms that, done well, performed the same cultural work as the nineteenth-century social novel, but with better pacing.

So, while searching for balance in my life, I tried my hand at crime fiction and found that I could escape into a different part of my imagination, so that I could go back to the library refreshed, our local dramas put into their proper perspective. Writing fiction also gave me a chance to get to know something about the trade publishing industry at a time of great upheaval, led me to connect with avid readers and delve into scholarship on the reading experience (fascinating stuff), and has given me an excuse to research all kinds of odd things: the history of surveillance of dissidents in America, the emotional aftereffects of sexual violence, the psychology of false eyewitness, and how communities respond to moral panics, not to mention the pesky minutia of whether a particular police organization uses jacketed or hollow-point bullets or what kind of search warrant would be needed for a totally fictional situation.

It just occurred to me that's something we get when we graduate with an MLS: a search warrant.

One of the other effects of our reorganization was that every librarian at my place of work became more involved in the big picture. We all began to teach, because it's too important a function to leave to one person. We all would build the collection and make budget decisions together. We'd each take turns serving in the role that in most libraries is reserved for a director and share the decision-making involved. This gave us all an opportunity to learn new things and to see how all of these activities fit together to make a library a place for learning.

Delving into budget spreadsheets and thinking about the priorities that guide budget allocations was a revelation. I became fascinated by the culture and commerce around scholarly publishing. I had first heard of the serials crisis in 1980, when earning my MLS at the University of Texas. The head of collection development had to break the news to the campus that there would be a painful but necessary trimming of periodical subscriptions. She showed me her charts; if prices kept going on, in a few short years the university libraries would have no budget for books. Though at the time the university system seemed to be floating effortlessly on oil revenues from the Permian Basin (which kept tuition amazingly low), the trend lines pointed clearly to a crisis, one we're still dealing with. Budgets are down, increased "productivity" in terms of numbers of publications is the measure of our worth, and the rapid transmission of information on the Internet has ironically made it even easier for a few giant corporations to corner a growing piece of the scholarly publishing market, earning profit margins that are shameful, turning research written to be shared into corporate property, refashioning themselves as the archivists and providers of knowledge, making libraries merely local purchasing agents.

But we don't have to go along. We don't need to sustain a publishing model that depends on subscriptions and licenses. There's no question information comes at a cost, but we can rethink how we sustain it and, at the same time, make it more universally available—which, if you think about it, is what our values tell us to do.

So once again, here were are, peering over the horizon. We know what libraries are for, and merely paying the bills for consumption is not it. We can work with scholars and with fugitives from an increasingly dysfunctional publishing industry to build something new and better, and I'm confident we will. There are too many options available today build something better, and too much at stake.

For me, though, the real purpose of all of this—the teaching we do, the collections we organize, and the role we will play in the future of scholarship—is the cultivation of voices and the ensemble that we form in conversation together. I find myself returning, again and again, to a passage by philosopher Michael Oakeshott in his essay "The Voice of Poetry in the Conversation of Mankind," encountered in my first year as a full-time librarian. It seemed true then, and true today.

> Voices which speak in conversation do not compose a hierarchy. Conversation is not an enterprise designed to yield an extrinsic profit, a contest where a winner gets a prize, nor is it an activity of exegesis; it is an unrehearsed intellectual adventure... we are the inheritors, neither of an inquiry about ourselves and the world, nor of an accumulating body of information, but of a conversation, begun in the primeval forests and extended and made more articulate in the course of centuries. It is a conversation that goes on both in public and within each of ourselves... Education, properly speaking, is an initiation into the skill and partnership of this conversation in which we learn to recognize the voices, to distinguish the proper occasions of utterance, and in which we acquire the intellectual and moral habits appropriate to conversation. And it is this conversation which, in the end, gives place and character to every human activity and utterance.[3]

NOTES

1. T. Scott Plutchak, "Breaking the Barriers of Time and Space: The Dawning of the Great Age of Librarians." *Journal of the Medical Library Association: JMLA* 100, no. 1 (January 2012) 10-19.
2. Nina Sankovitch,. *Tolstoy and the Purple Chair: My Year of Magical Reading.* (New York: HarperCollins, 2011) 20.
3. Joseph Michael Oakeshott, "The Voice of Poetry in the Conversation of Mankind," In *Rationalism in Politics and Other Essays,* (New York: Basic) 198-199.

BIBLIOGRAPHY

Oakeshott, Michael Joseph. "The Voice of Poetry in the Conversation of Mankind." *Rationalism in Politics and Other Essays.* New York, New York: Basic, 197-247.

Plutchak, T. Scott. "Breaking the Barriers of Time and Space: The Dawning of the Great Age of Librarians." *Journal of the Medical Library Association : JMLA* 100, no. 1 (January 2012): 10–19. doi:10.3163/1536-5050.100.1.004.

Sankovitch, Nina. *Tolstoy and the Purple Chair: My Year of Magical Reading.* New York, New York: HarperCollins, 2011.

Section I

Change and Academic Librarians

Academic Librarianship and Career Adaptability

Tara Baillargeon
Head, Research and Instructional Services, Raynor Memorial Libraries, Marquette University

Aaron Carlstrom
Clinical Assistant Professor, Psychology Department, University of Wisconsin-Parkside

We were inspired to write this essay by Barbara Fister's assertion that, in order to support the user's need for information, librarians must embrace functions that have not traditionally been in the academic librarian's portfolio. We shall examine the need for career adaptability in librarianship, and use a case study to illustrate four attributes librarians must develop to ensure career adaptability. The case study involved collaboration between Kansas State University (KSU) Libraries; Dr. Chuck Rice, a KSU agronomy professor; and the Global Research Alliance on Agricultural Greenhouse Gases (an international research group focused on growing food while reducing greenhouse gas emissions), to develop an open access croplands research database. We will draw from vocational psychology to discuss career adaptability, and outline strategies librarians can use to nurture and maintain career concern, career control, career curiosity and career confidence (4 Cs).[1]

Introduction

All academic librarians made a series of decisions that led to their current position. They attended college; chose an undergraduate major;

pursued a graduate degree in library science; and focused on an area within academic librarianship. To make these decisions, they likely relied on self-knowledge (e.g., interests, skills, needs, values, supports and challenges from other life roles) and what they understood about a librarian's work (e.g., professional responsibilities, skills, training and educational requirements, rewards and compensation, challenges, influence on lifestyle). They gathered this information from many resources, such as online and print sources; career self-assessments; volunteer and work experience; informational interviews; professional organizations; career counselors and advisors; academic courses; and family, friends, mentors and supervisors. Many likely found academic librarianship to be a good match because the job met their professional needs (e.g., liking and being good at their job duties, interacting with people in ways they enjoy) and personal needs (e.g., work schedules that provide time to spend on hobbies, with friends and family, and engaged in their community).

However, the needs of individuals, and of disciplines and occupations, do change over time. Academic librarians may face more significant changes today than in previous years, in large part because of globalization, shifting demographics, and significant advances in information technology.[2] Consequently, academic librarians must acquire and use new skills and knowledge, and deploy current skills and knowledge in new ways if the profession is to remain relevant and successfully respond to faculty, students, administrators and other stakeholders. Although this evolution benefits the profession (and many primary responsibilities will remain unchanged) some academic librarians may feel uncertain and anxious, and question their competence and interest in this new environment. Thus, it is important to understand what helps individual academic librarians adapt to new roles and responsibilities, and simultaneously experience meaning and relevance. Furthermore, in the current climate, it is not enough to help people adapt to current shifts in the profession; we also need to understand how to best respond to future changes.

In 2010, the Association of College and Research Libraries (ACRL) published "Futures Thinking for Academic Librarians: Higher Education in 2025." Its authors assessed current trends in academia, and developed 26 scenarios that might represent the future in academic librarianship. Then, they surveyed ACRL members on their beliefs about each scenario's probability and impact. Even a casual perusing of the document will convey that academic librarianship is changing rapidly. One of the scenarios identified by respondents as highly probable with high impact is a bridging of the scholar/practitioner divide. In this scenario, open peer-review will become the norm. This, in turn, will support community-based dialogue, and scholars and practitioners will be able to discuss how research findings apply to practice. One survey respondent wrote,

> Libraries will need to reconsider what their relevance is in the research process. We need to start considering what our 'deeper meaning' is to researchers to ensure that we fit into this new model. I feel strongly that we will have a role - it will look different from our role now, and we need to be careful not to cling to past practice for nostalgic reasons.[3]

Essential to this new model are librarians whose adaptability to changes to the profession will ensure their professional success as individuals, and contribute to enhancing librarianship's value to research.

ACRL has not been alone in predicting changes in academic librarianship. The Taiga Forum, comprised of university library deans from large institutions, prepares librarians for meaningful leadership roles in the field. The Forum is best known for an annual list of "provocative statements" about the future of academic libraries. In 2011, they predicted that a new model of liaison librarianship, focused on institutional content, would emerge in five years. Two years later, this is already happening. Librarians are increasingly focused on collaborations with faculty in teaching and research efforts, and are spending less time answering questions at the reference desk.

Furthermore, the work of liaison librarians is changing, even for those who entered the work force as little as five years ago. There are growing expectations among funders, such as the National Institutes of Health, that research be interdisciplinary, data-intensive, and collaborative, requiring researchers to develop interdisciplinary teams.[4] With these moves away from siloed research, librarians too, must find ways to adapt new models of research, and support the creation and discoverability of institutional content. Career adaptability is essential for librarians to be successful and find fulfillment over the course of their careers.

The Four Dimensions (4 Cs) of Career Adaptability

Career adaptability[5] provides a framework for understanding how librarians might find fulfillment as their roles change, and relies on the "readiness and resources" to cope with "vocational development tasks, occupational transitions, and personal traumas."[6] There are four dimensions to career adaptability—career concern, career control, career curiosity, career confidence—and each speaks to attitudes, beliefs, competencies, and behaviors that serve as coping strategies, and indicate openness to career transitions. In this chapter, we explore how academic librarians can develop the readiness, resources, and strategies to manage occupational transitions in a rapidly changing profession, accountable to a variety of stakeholders.

Academic librarians with an adaptive level of *career concern* are those who are or are "becoming *concerned* about their future as a worker,"[7] in general, or as an academic librarian, specifically. This is not the same as disabling anxiety or worry, but instead involves an attitude or belief that *planning* for the future is necessary and beneficial. Career adaptive academic librarians cope with occupational transitions by being *aware*, and by anticipating transitions in roles and responsibilities in their own careers and throughout the profession. These librarians maintain beliefs and attitudes that allow them to make good choices, and *prepare* for the future by being *involved* in activities that accomplish today's work tasks, and those anticipated in the future.[8] By connecting the present to the future—in thought and action—one can experience continuity as the profession evolves. These librarians become able to see the differences between the profession they originally prepared for and what it has become, but they are not personally disrupted by this awareness because they act on the themes that connect the two.

Career control is assuming "*control* over (one's) vocational future."[9] This means that one feels *responsible* for their vocational future, and thus, is able to make *autonomous* career plans and choices. To have this control, people must be competent *decision makers*. Career adaptive academic librarians are able to be *assertive, disciplined* and *willful* when coping with transitions.[10] This is not a call for extreme individualism, but recognition that people are more likely to experience work-satisfaction after professional transitions when they take ownership of their career paths, instead of leaving them to chance. In this process, some will act independently and others more interdependently. There are parameters on these choices, especially when one wishes to remain in a changing profession, and with an employer. Nevertheless, exercising career control can assist in positive adaptation. People should always review the choices they have; make intentional choices; and take responsibility for their work.[11]

Academic librarians display *career curiosity*, "... by exploring possible selves and future scenarios" (p. 52) because they believe it is beneficial to be *inquisitive* about their profession (e.g., "What is changing in academic libraries, and at my institution?") and themselves (e.g., "Which of these changes excites me the most?"). To be curious in this way, people must be competent *explorers*, or nimble information-gatherers. There are many resources to aid this kind of professional development, such as journals; professional organizations; colleagues; supervisors; mentors; and events and activities. Career adaptive librarians manage career transitions by gathering information about the profession, their institutions, and noticing where these categories overlap and diverge. Furthermore, they *take risks* and experiment with different professional roles and tasks.[12]

It is also important that academic librarians have or develop "... the *confidence* to pursue their aspirations"[13] and believe they are able to achieve goals, negotiate challenges, and overcome obstacles. Librarians must feel like they are able to achieve broad career aspirations, and feel confident taking on specific responsibilities in a job description. For example, an academic librarian may feel confident in her ability to eventually become a department head, but not feel confident about her ability to contribute to a faculty member's proposal for a large, international research grant. When pursuing their professional aspirations, career adaptive academic librarians cope with career transitions by *persisting, striving* and being *industrious.*[14] Being career adaptive requires competent *problem solving*.

As academic librarians negotiate the gaps between the profession they entered (or believed they entered), and the one they find themselves in, different people will have different (and adaptive) levels of career concern, control, curiosity and confidence because of age, professional experiences, and number of years in the profession. Institutional and societal barriers—including discrimination—can influence career adaptability. Also, individual characteristics (such as level of openness to new experiences, motivation, anxiousness) and institutional assets (such as availability of mentors, administrative support, institutional resources, opportunities for advancement or lateral position changes) will influence the development of the four dimensions of career adaptability.

Case Study in Career Adaptability: Collaborating to Develop an Open Access Database

Overview

In 2009, Kansas State University Libraries embarked on a reorganization of library staff in an effort to better address user needs, adapt to changes in library collections, and reallocate resources to new, developing areas in librarianship. One outcome of the reorganization the creation of a new department called Faculty and Graduate Services (FGS); their mission was, in part, to form collaborative partnerships with faculty and enhance research. To get a better understanding of research activities occurring on campus, and identify potential roles for the library, FGS librarians made an effort get out of their offices to network at campus research meetings. At one meeting, FGS librarians began discussions with Dr. Chuck Rice, a KSU agronomy professor, on how the libraries might collaborate with him and support his work for the Global Research Alliance (GRA) on Agricultural Greenhouse Gasses. (Rice was a U.S. representative to the GRA, a global alliance of more than 30 countries established after a United Nations Climate Change Conference in 2009.) Dr. Rice and his GRA colleagues identified the need for an open access database of literature and data to assist croplands and greenhouse gases researchers all over the world. Once he and the FGS librarians decided to create a database on greenhouse gas emissions generated by croplands, the Croplands Research Database pilot[15] was born.

The team determined that the best approach to creating the database was to start small. Dr. Rice was already working closely with an Australian GRA Croplands colleague, so the project team decided to begin with research generated from the United States and Australia. This way they had opportunities to remedy problems before making the site live. For instance, they could identify and correct any copyright issues, understand editing challenges, and set up an efficient work flow procedure that international colleagues could follow.

The Libraries and GRA Croplands Group members agreed that the database would contain published research, grey papers, reviews, and synopses. After the first phase of the project, GRA group members would be able to input their own content into the database.[16] The group members and library partners wished to make sure this collated information was not available elsewhere, to enhance the value of this pilot project.

Career Adaptability and Timing

Career adaptability involves adjusting to new job tasks and career transitions "by solving problems that are usually unfamiliar, often ill-defined, and always complex."[17] The opportunity to develop the GRA Croplands database emerged after the Libraries underwent a large restructuring, and the FGS department was established. This Department was still seeking an identity and working to define its collective goals, but most FGS members already had experience as subject liaisons, responsible for instruction, collection development, and reference services for their assigned departments. In the new model, librarians were expected to focus more on building collaborative relationships with faculty and graduate students in teaching and research. To be successful, librarians would need to re-envision their roles, learn new skills, and do new things.

The database offered such an opportunity. Neither of the project librarians involved had experience developing a research database from the ground up. Not only was database creation a new skill, but croplands research was a new subject area for the librarians. Fortunately, expertise in croplands was not necessary for the database to be successful—the GRA researchers brought extensive subject knowledge to the project. Instead, the librarians' roles were to design the final project with Dr. Rice, manage the process, and import, clean, and organize the data. Additional library staff members provided the programming support for website development, graphic design, and server space. The pilot project resulted in the creation of a browsable and searchable croplands research database containing research from over 30 countries (available at http://www.lib.k-state.edu/gracroplands).

The 4 Cs of Career Adaptability

The reorganization of KSU's Libraries was, essentially, inspired by *career concern* about academic librarianship, and librarians' changing roles. Budget constraints, technological advances, and the changing landscape of information necessitated the library to assess their role on campus. Librarians knew they provided crucial support to research, teaching, and learning on campus, but they needed to leverage their strengths to do it most effectively. The reassessment led to the restructuring of the departments, priorities, and goals of the library, including the creation of the Faculty and Graduate Services Department.

During the library's reorganization, new departments including the Faculty and Graduate Services Department were created, providing an opportunity for librarians to practice *career control*. Librarians were able to increase their control over the future by deciding what work they wanted to do and in which department their work could be accomplished. Librarians who chose to work in the Faculty and Graduate Services department decided that their futures involved collaborating with and supporting the work of faculty and graduate students on campus. They were librarians willing to be partners in grant writing, creating digital collections, scholarly publishing, and assessing research impact. For many of the librarians these activities required them to take initiative to learn about work that was new to them. Few of the librarians had extensive experience collaborating on grant proposals or knew exactly what it meant to support the assessment of a faculty member's research impact.

By leaving their offices to attend campus research meetings, departmental brown bag sessions, and other campus events, librarians working on the GRA Croplands project demonstrated *career curiosity*. Their participation informed librarians of current and emerging research projects, and encouraged them to think of other ways (besides traditional research consultations) they might support research. Notably, the librarians first met Dr. Rice at such an event, an example of "planned happenstance." After all, professional success is not always the result of carefully made plans; it is often the product of one's ability to be open-minded, follow personal interests, and capitalize on chance events.[18]

Finally, librarians make easier career adaptations when they anticipate their own success, and have *career confidence* in their ability to overcome obstacles. To participate in the GRA Croplands project, the librarians had to overcome fears of having inadequate skills or knowledge, and take risks by participating in something new.

Development of Career Adaptability in Librarians

People with low levels of career concern, control, curiosity and confidence can develop greater career adaptability by accessing support through networking opportunities and information (such as supervisory and mentoring relationships), and by attending workshops and other professional development activities. However, some individuals with career challenges face more serious personal and environmental obstacles that are not ameliorated by encouragement, support, networking opportunities, and information.

Career indifference may be experienced by those with low levels of career concern.[19] Librarians with career indifference tend to be pessimistic about the future and avoid longer-term career planning. *Orientation exercises,* such as attending workshops or conferences focusing on the future of libraries, can be helpful for librarians experiencing career indifference.[20] Professional organizations, such as ACRL, publish articles and white papers about the future of librarianship and can serve as valuable resources for information and networking. It is also helpful to have at least one library mentor who can help set goals, ensuring that he or she takes action now to make sure those future goals are met.

Those with low levels of career control experience may *career indecision,* which makes it very difficult to make choices about future career paths.[21] Instead of planning for the future, they continue to only focus on their current routines. *Decisional training,* teaching people how to make plans and complete the necessary steps, can be helpful for people with career indecision.[22] It is possible that a librarian with career indecision lacks information and feels overwhelmed with the choices ahead, especially in such a rapidly changing environment. Again, mentors can provide help and clarity.

Those with low levels of career curiosity may experience *career unrealism,* and hold unrealistic views of librarianship and how to be successful at work.[23] This may involve librarians thinking that the work they are doing right now is fine and there is no need to change anything. Career unrealism indicates a lack of understanding about librarianship, and may indicate a fear of change. *Information-seeking activities,* such as attending lectures, attending conferences, and developing relationships with mentors who can help them think proactively, can be helpful for those with career unrealism.[24]

Finally, those with low levels of career confidence may experience *career inhibition*, which occurs when people do not believe they have the ability to change or problem solve.[25] Librarians with career inhibition may see that libraries are evolving, and know they have to make changes, but they do not think they can do it. *Confidence building* can be helpful for these librarians.[26] Supervisors can help with confidence building by having clear expectations, and offering praise when warranted. Working with human resources departments to provide trainings and skill-building sessions also may boost staff confidence and competencies.

Conclusion

The roles of librarians are changing. In this chapter, we focus on strategies academic librarians can use to remain flexible, positive, and adapt to changing roles and responsibilities, with the goal of continued tenure at their current institutions. We hope this process is helpful, and aids librarians who may feel anxious or worried in the changing climate. However, after reflecting on current and future personal needs, as well as those of the profession and institution; taking responsibility for the course their career takes; exploring career possibilities; and developing the confidence to respond to changes and achieve the career they want; an academic librarian may decide to seek work at another institution, or switch professions.

In *Reframing Academic Leadership*, Bolman and Gallos (2011) remind us of the need to seek opportunities for growth:

> Don't be afraid to experiment—stretching oneself broadens life and work skills. It can be risky: you may not learn as quickly as needed, and you can find yourself in over your head. Think carefully before you leap, and then keep an open mind. We learn from failure as well as success, and sometimes learning is even easier when the going is rough.[27]

NOTES

1. Mark Savickas. "The theory and practice of career construction." In *Career Development and Counseling: Putting Theory and Research to Work*. (Hoboken, NJ: John Wiley & Sons, 2005).

2. R. Feller and J. Whichard, *Knowledge Nomads and the Nervously Employed: Workplace Change & Courageous Career Choices*. CAPS Press, 2005.

3. David Staley and Kara Malenfant, "Futures Thinking for Academic Librarians: Higher Education in 2025. Association of College and Research Libraries," *Association of College and Research Libraries*, 2005, http://www.ala.org/acrl/sites/ala.org.acrl/files/content/issues/value/futures2025.pdf.

4. "The NIH Common Fund Office of Strategic Communication," National Institutes of Health, 2012, https://commonfund.nih.gov/interdisciplinary/index.aspx; "Rebuilding the Mosaic: Fostering Research in the Social, Behavioral, and Economic Sciences at the National Science Foundation in the Next Decade," *National Science Foundation, Directorate for Social, Behavioral and Economic Sciences*, 2011, http://www.nsf.gov/pubs/2011/nsf11086/nsf11086.pdf.

5. Mark Savickas. "The theory and practice of career construction." In *Career Development and Counseling: Putting Theory and Research to Work*. (Hoboken, NJ: John Wiley & Sons, 2005).

6. Ibid., .51.

7. Ibid., .52.

8. Ibid.

9. Ibid., .51.

10. Ibid., .52.

11. Ibid.

12. Ibid.

13. Ibid.

14. Ibid.

15. Livia Olsen, Tara Baillargeon, and Harish Maringanti, "Developing an Open Access Croplands Research Database through Global Collaboration," *Journal of Agricultural and Food Information* 13, no. 1 (2012) : 35-44.

16. "Croplands Research Group Final Meeting Report," *Global Research Alliance on Agricultural Greenhouse Gases*, INRA Grignon and Palais de Congress de Versailles, France, March 2011, http://www.ricclisa.org/informacion-general.

17. Ibid.

18. K.E. Mitchell, Al Levin, and J.D. Krumboltz, "Planned Happenstance: Constructing Unexpected Career Opportunities," *Journal of Counseling & Development*, 77 (1999) : 115–124.

19. Ibid.

20. Ibid.

21. Ibid.

22. Ibid.

23. Ibid.

24. Ibid.

25. Ibid.

26. Ibid.

27. L.G. Bolman and J.V. Gallos, *Reframing Academic Leadership*, (San Francisco: Jossey-Bass, 2011).

REFERENCES

Bolman, L. G., and J.V. Gallos, *Reframing Academic Leadership*. San Francisco: Jossey-Bass, 2011.

Dotlich, D.L., Noel, J. L. and Walker, N., "Learning for Leadership: Failure as a Second Change." In *Business Leadership* edited by J.V. Gallos, pp. 478-483. San Francisco: Jossey Bass, 2008.

Feller, R., and Whichard, J. *Knowledge nomads and the nervously employed: Workplace change & courageous career choices*. CAPS Press, 2005.

Global Research Alliance on Agricultural Greenhouse Gases. (2011). Croplands Research Group Final Meeting Report. INRA Grignon and Palais de Congress de Versailles, France, March 2011. Retrieved from http://www.ricclisa.org/informacion-general

Mitchell, K. E., Al Levin, S., & Krumboltz, J. D. (1999), Planned Happenstance: Constructing Unexpected Career Opportunities. Journal of Counseling & Development, 77: 115–124. doi: 10.1002/j.1556-6676.1999.tb02431.x

National Institutes of Health. The NIH Common Fund Office of Strategic Communication. (2012). Interdisciplinary Research. Retrieved from https://commonfund.nih.gov/interdisciplinary/index.aspx.

National Science Foundation, Directorate for Social, Behavioral and Economic Sciences. (2011). Rebuilding the Mosaic: Fostering Research in the Social, Behavioral, and Economic Sciences at the National Science Foundation in the Next Decade. Arlington, VA: National Science Foundation NSF 11-086. Retrieved From http://www.nsf.gov/pubs/2011/nsf11086/nsf11086.pdf.

Olsen, L., Baillargeon, T., and Maringanti, H., "Developing an Open Access Croplands Research Database through Global Collaboration." *Journal of Agricultural and Food Information* 13, no. 1 (2012) : 35-44. http://www.tandfonline.com/doi/abs/10.1080/10496505.2012.639272

Staley, David J. and Malenfant, Kara J. (2010). Futures Thinking for Academic Librarians: Higher Education in 2025. Association of College and Research Libraries. Available at http://www.ala.org/acrl/sites/ala.org.acrl/files/content/issues/value/futures2025.pdf

Missouri Universities, Librarians, and Accreditation:

A Survey of Librarians' Involvement in the Self-study Processes

Laurie Hathman
Director, Greenlease Library, Rockhurst University

Danielle Theiss
Head of Public Services, Greenlease Library, Rockhurst University

Colleges and universities undergo a cyclical process of external peer review, something that can be referred to as organizational quality control. These reviews, conducted by external and objective organizations, are essential for federal funding streams to remain viable. They guarantee the validity of the degrees conferred upon students at graduation, and enable institutions to secure financial support from donors. These reviews also systematically reveal how institutions compare to each other, with regard to academic programs, financial stability, student services and other criteria.

Barbara Fister noted in the article *What Do They Know: Assessing the Library's Contribution to Student Learning* that, "because of a growing perception that the public demands accountability, the influence of market models on higher education that position education as a product and students as consumers..."[1] Institutions of higher education face increasing demands to demonstrate to external constituents institutional, program-matic, and student learning achievement. All institutions are held to the same evaluative standards. This systematic quality control process is re-ferred to as accreditation. Within the United States a national governing agency manages the accreditation of all universities, colleges, and trade schools. To effectively do this, there are regional organizations which man-age certain geographic zones.

Higher education institutions in Missouri fall under the jurisdiction of the Higher Learning Commission of the North Central Association of Colleges and Schools. Institutions are evaluated on a cyclical basis, usually every ten years, although these timelines are currently being reconsidered. For example, the institution used in this chapter as the case study, Rockhurst University, recently underwent a reaffirmation of continuing accreditation in 2012. Its previous review cycle was ten years ago, in 2002. Rockhurst University, a private Jesuit and Catho-lic university is located in Kansas City, Missouri, has an FTE of 2,320 students, and is designated as a Master's Colleges and Universities I in-stitution under the Carnegie Classification Code. The library has four full-time librarians, 167,462 print volumes and 6,156 e-book volumes.[2] There are also specialized accrediting agencies for certain academic disciplines or programs. For example, the Association of Advance Col-legiate Schools of Business (AACSB) accredits business schools, and the Commission on Collegiate Nursing Education (CCNE) accredits nursing programs.[3,4]

As part of this systematic review process, universities undergo their own internal review, or self-study, leading up to an external review from outside evaluators. This paper will examine the self-study process involvement of Missouri academic libraries at institutions which received reaffirmation of continuing accreditation between the years 2006-2012. A case study of one institution's self-study process and the library's involvement (Rock-hurst University) will also be shared.

Purpose of the Self-study: Peer Review

As part of the peer review process, institutions undergo an internal review, or an institutional self-study. One component of the self-study is a detailed narrative outlining how the institution successfully meets criteria established by the outside accrediting agency. In the case of the Higher Learning Commission, and the basis of all the institutions discussed in this paper, there are five criteria with multiple core components[5]:

- Criterion One: Mission and Integrity
- Criterion Two: Preparing for the Future
- Criterion Three: Student Learning and Effective Teaching
- Criterion Four: Acquisition, Discovery, and Application of Knowledge
- Criterion Five: Engagement and Service

The Higher Learning Commission offers strategies for an effective self-study, noting that it builds its evaluation and recommendations based on two things: the institutional self-study and peer evaluation, usually accomplished through an on-campus accreditation team visit. The institution can utilize these strategies as it crafts its self-study report, demonstrating how the criteria are exemplified in its current academic processes. An effective self-study process contains the following:

- It fits the distinctive nature of the organization.
- It achieves stated goals that guide the design and the conduct of the process.
- It ensures effective evaluation of the whole institution.
- It promises to have an impact on the institution beyond the Commission visit.
- It engages multiple constituencies of the institution.
- It builds naturally on existing and ongoing self-evaluation processes.
- It has strong presidential and board support.
- It draws on the expertise and credibility of recognized leaders throughout the institution.

- It maintains regular and effective communication links with institutional constituencies.
- It produces evidence to show that the Commission's Criteria for Accreditation are met.
- It produces a self-study report that meets the Commission's needs.
- It testifies to the institution's commitment to peer review.[6]

H. R. Kells provides additional guidance for institutions as they prepare for the self-study process, and a rubric for analyzing the overall process in his book *Self-study Processes: A Guide to Self-Evaluation in Higher Education*. Kells offers self-study organizational schemes, self-evaluation processes and designs, and general overview steps to the process. The first step is to form a small group to diagnose the situation, and offer design strategies. After the design of the self-study process is developed, it must be organized by defining relevant stakeholders, including roles, tasks, and timelines. Working groups and communication mechanisms must be established, before the self-study is conducted. Then, the working group collects facts and opinions; surveys stakeholders and the community; discusses the results; and prepares the report. The external reviewers are hosted by the institution, and offer feedback and recommendations. The institution initiates follow-up activities, and reviews the self-study process at their campus.[7]

In a 1987 study, Mary Casserly drew from Kells' recommendations and directions, and examined how academic libraries were supporting their institutional self-study processes when she evaluated four libraries at institutions that completed their self-studies between 1978-1980.[8] Casserly assessed these libraries and their self-study experiences, especially examining tangible outcomes (establishment of ongoing institutional research, self-analysis, a clearly written self-study report, and improvements in library functioning during or after the study) and organizational or personal benefits. Questions falling under the category of "Motivation" or "Commitment" measured whether the survey respondent viewed the self-study as a method to improve the library, and if library and institution leaders demonstrated commitment to the self-study.

Casserly's findings suggest that three out of the four institutions surveyed viewed the self-study as a way of improving the library. Staff at institutions which had enjoyed positive self-study experiences fully expected to make changes based on the self-evaluation findings. While librarian participation in the self-study processes of their institutions varied in Casserly's study, institutions which had more successful self-study outcomes incorporated more participation by librarians. For example, Casserly notes that, "at sites A and B, the librarians played only limited roles in the self-study process. In contrast, participation in the process by the librarians at the successful sites was widespread... At site D, the librarians participated in the self-study process by contributing their opinions on library strength and weaknesses, providing data... and reviewing and commenting on the report..."[9] Additionally, Casserly found that librarians who had prior experience with self-study processes, or accreditation-related activities, often rated their self-study current process as more successful. While Casserly focused solely on library self-studies, the authors of this essay focused on the roles librarians played in institutional accreditation activities. Casserly graciously agreed to share her survey methodology and questions, and we were able to adapt our questions from her work.

Missouri and Academic Librarians' Roles

What is the role that Missouri academic librarians have played in their university or college's reaffirmation of continued accreditation self-study process?

Methodology

Drawing from M.F. Casserly's study on accreditation-related self-study as a planned change process, the authors conducted a similar study targeting 27 Missouri higher education library deans or directors. The authors inquired about the role of the academic librarian in their most recent accreditation, as well as how the participants viewed the self-study process in general. The institutions chosen had received a reaffirmation of continuing accreditation by the Higher Learning Commission from 2006-2012, and ranged from small for-profit specialty colleges to large research institutions. All libraries served institutions with an FTE between 116 to 10,155 and employed between 1 and 24 librarians. Print collections of the survey participants' libraries range in size from 22,285 to 1,228,382 volumes. E-books held at the institutions varied from 0 volumes held to 56,971 volumes. Four of the institutions were classified under the Carnegie classification code as Associate Colleges, four as Baccalaureate Colleges, three as Master's Colleges or Universities I or II, two as Doctoral/Research Universities-Intensive, three as separate Health Profession schools, four as Theological Seminaries and one as a Teacher's College.[10] The data for this study was collected using an online survey. The web-based survey was sent individually to the library director or dean of the library at the institution. Thirteen of the twenty-seven institutions surveyed responded to the eight question survey form with an overall response rate of forty-eight percent.

The survey was divided in two sections: Part I gauged the participant's familiarity of the self-study process, and Part II the involvement of the library or librarians with the self-study process at the institution. Demographic questions were included regarding the respondents length of employment at the time of the most recent reaffirmation of continuing accreditation. Additional survey questions asked respondents to report their direct involvement with the self-study process; if they felt that they learned more about the institution; or if conducting the self-study changed any process or procedure at their institution.

Survey Findings
Roles and Experience in a Self-Study Process
At the time of their self-study, the roles and length of service of the survey participants varied at their institutions (figure 2.1).

Eight self-identified as Library Directors, two as Deans of the Learning Resource Center, and one as an associate professor. Fifty-four percent of the respondents had worked at their institutions more than ten years.

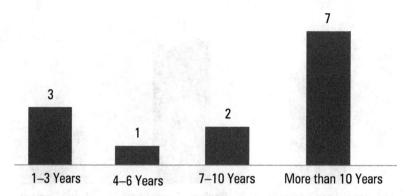

Figure 2.1. Length of Employment in Position at Time of Self-study Process

To establish a baseline, the survey respondents were asked where they had become familiar with the self-study process (figure 2.2).

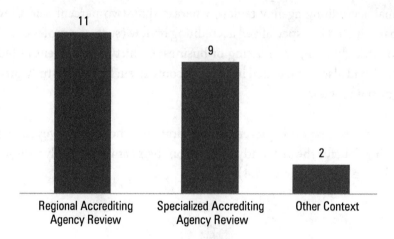

Figure 2.2. Context of Self-study Familiarity

Eighty-five percent of respondents noted that this familiarity came from their participation in regional accrediting agency reviews, whereas only fifteen percent said either specialized accreditation reviews or some other context.

Librarians who actively participated in a self-study did so in a variety of ways (figure 2.3).

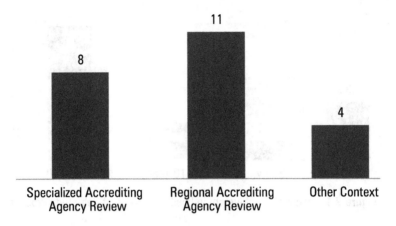

Figure 2.3. Self-study Process Context of Experience

Eighty-five percent of respondents noted that they had participated in a regional accrediting agency review, whereas sixty-two percent said they had participated in a specialized accrediting review (such as a professional school accreditation, like nursing or business). Thirty-one percent noted that they had also participated in another context, such as a self-study process, or state reviews.

Overall, the primary role played by the librarians who were surveyed was providing data for the self-study to those on their campus directly responsible for the process (figure 2.4).

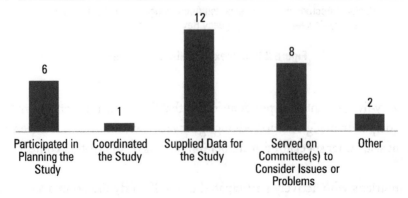

Figure 2.4. Librarians' Role in Self-study Process

Ninety-two percent of the respondents identified that role. Sixty-two percent served on a committee to consider problems or issues related to the
self-study and forty-six percent were deeply involved in the self-study. This
included an individual who served as a coordinator of the self-study, one
who was the organizer of the Higher Learning Commission's Resource
Room, and another as a writer/editor of the self-study report (figure 2.5).

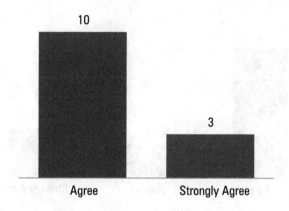

Figure 2.5. Self-study Process is a Technique for Improving the Institution

Actionable Outcomes of the Self-study Process

Given the expectation of accrediting agencies that the self-study process will
result in institutional change, the survey asked several questions regarding
whether the self-study process was perceived as improving the institution.

All participants believed the self-study process was a technique for improving the institution, with seventy-seven percent of respondents rating the
question at "agree," and an additional twenty-three percent strongly agree-
ing with this statement. For example, one survey respondent stated, "the
writer/editors of the study were privy to very close examination of all materials included, and since the Dean of the library was among the writers, this
information has had far- reaching impacts on the nature and effectiveness
of library services within the College." Another responded "in general, the
library has received very positive feedback during accreditation visits that
follow the self-study process. While this is reassuring, it also tends to gener-

ate the feeling that the library does not have additional needs—which is not the case." This may lead to a sense that future changes are not needed for certain departments or schools if they fair positively during the review process.

We were interested in also knowing if the self-study process was perceived as a useful tool in strategic planning of institutional change, policies, or procedures (figure 2.6).

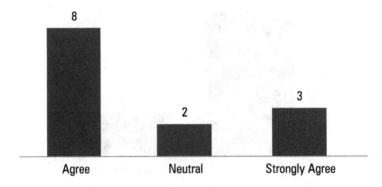

Figure 2.6. Self-study Process is a Tool for Institutional Planning

Eighty-five percent responded that they agreed or strongly agreed that this was so. However, one respondent noted "The institution continues to struggle to connect planning with the budget process." Participants were asked how they perceived the use of institutional resources (staff members' time, monetary funds, etc.) in the self-study process (figure 2.7).

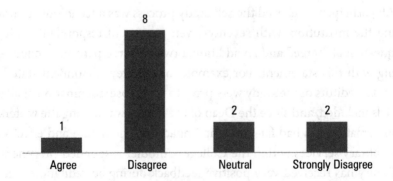

Figure 2.7. Self-study Process is a Wasteful Use of Institutional Resources

Asked if it was a wasteful use of resources, seventy-seven percent of the respondents disagreed or strongly disagreed with that statement. Fifteen percent chose neutral.

Those who were participants in a self-study process were asked if they considered it a meaningless exercise for the institution (figure 2.8).

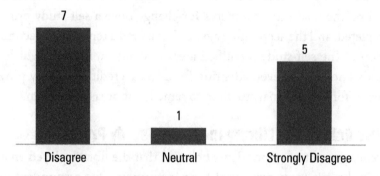

Figure 2.8. Self-study Process is a Meaningless Exercise

Ninety-two percent of respondents felt that the process was not meaningless with one participant neutral in response.

Respondents indicated that the self-study process was useful in evaluation of the institution (figure 2.9).

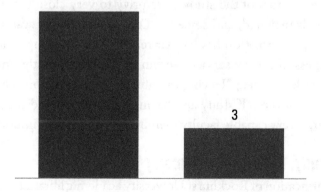

Figure 2.9. Self-Study Process is Useful

Eighty-five percent of respondents noted that the self-study process was useful, but fifteen percent saying that they were not sure if it was or not. For example, one respondent who believed the process was useful stated that the "self-study helped confirm much of what we knew or thought, and it helped identify or clarify a few things that facilitated prioritization, resource allocation, and further analysis. Self-study has become an ongoing process with annual assessment grids, feedback loops, etc." Another response centered on the institution's impetus for change once a self-study process is completed, and the accrediting agency has issued a report with recommendations. "The self-study identified areas of concern, many of which were already known; however, attention from the accrediting agency provided impetus for institutional attention to remedy the areas of concern."

Active Role of the Library in the Self-study Process

Seventy percent of respondents believed that the library played an active role in the self-study process at their institution. One respondent noted, "The latest self-study was conducted for an HLC visit in October 2011. This is the second HLC visit with which I was involved, and this time the effort was campus-wide. In addition to my library participation, I was tasked with organizing and managing the Resource Room, which gave me a very interesting perspective on the College." Another stated, "All full-time library staff was either responsible for producing information for the study, or was interviewed in order to provide information for the study. The writer/editors of the study were privy to very close examination of all materials included, and since the Dean of the library was among the writers, this information has had far reaching impacts on the nature and effectiveness of library services within the College." Lastly, another survey respondent noted, "Having the library represented on the executive committee for the self-study and having a library-focused subcommittee chaired by a very capable faculty member were both very important."

Case Study: Rockhurst University

The identification of Rockhurst University academic librarians as key players in the institution's Higher Learning Commission (HLC) accreditation process began in the early planning stages for the self-study process. The Vice President for Academic Affairs, who was responsible for organizing the self-study committees, asked the Library Director to co-chair the Criterion 4 committee to examine "Acquisition, Discovery and Application of Knowledge." In subsequent conversation about the organization of the self-study documents, the Library Director promoted the expertise of academic librarians in the organizing information, and the value that this expertise could contribute to the self-study process. After the Library Director suggested that an additional librarian be included on the committee responsible for establishing the required electronic resource room where self-study documents would be stored, the self-study organizer accepted this idea.

The original technology committee responsible for the electronic resource room would include a librarian, as well as staff from Rockhurst's information technology department. At the time of this decision, the librarian position assigned to this committee—the Head of Technical Services—was vacant. The Library Director revised the responsibilities of the vacant position to include the role in the accreditation process, and candidates for the position were carefully screened for skill sets that would include this new role for the position. The Library Director was mindful that not only would this librarian be involved in creating the electronic resource room, but it was likely that they would also play a role after the electronic resource room opened. A successful candidate was identified and hired before the official work of the self-study process began.

The Library Director initially believed that the participation of two librarians would likely be sufficient allocation of library staff resources during the process, with other library staff providing support as needed. The steering committee timeline indicated that the workload would be spread out among five criterion committees, with two other committees responsible respectively for technology and writing the final draft of the self-study. Since the process would take more than two years from beginning to end, and the number of library staff was limited, the Library Director expected that others in the library would temporarily take on some responsibilities of the Head of Technical Services position to support the self-study.

Other initiatives the Library Director hoped to personally accomplish might also be delayed until the self-study process was completed. Therefore, goals and objectives for the upcoming two years were adjusted to include the self-study process. The Library Director anticipated that the largest time commitment would be required in the final year preceding the accreditation site team visit. The Library Director also believed additional staff resources would be needed in the final six months of the process, as intensive preparations for the electronic resource room would likely occur at that point.

Following the established pattern of open communication among the library staff, all staff were updated on a regular basis regarding the progress of the work on the self-study, and the value of the self-study process to the role of the library in the university. Ideas or concerns about its impact on the library were solicited, and appreciation was expressed for the support they were giving to the librarians directly involved.

During the first year of self-study process, a public services librarian retired and the librarian responsible for the electronic resource room was appointed Head of Public Services. Since the self-study process relied upon the skill set of this librarian, the Library Director revised the Head of Public Services position to include the self-study process, so the librarian would maintain her role in the process. The early experience of the librarians in the beginning stages of the self-study process reinforced the importance of the technology skill set in the previously vacant Head of Technical Services position. This was also a key consideration in the hiring of a new librarian into that position. This early flexibility for shifting responsibilities would prove to add valuable assistance in the final months of the self-study process, as library staff resources had to be stretched to accommodate the increasing work of the self-study.

In their roles as chairs of self-study committees, the librarians concentrated the first full year of the self-study on gathering institutional evidence, writing an initial draft as part of a criterion committee, and designing the electronic platform to house the evidence for the internal use of documents. Besides the two librarians and a member of the IT department, a co-chair of the self-study steering committee was involved in the early discussions for the electronic platform. Once the group decided to use Microsoft SharePoint as the platform, the Head of Technical Services, as Chair of the Technology and Communication committee for the self-study, did the detailed work in SharePoint. This included developing fields, an input form, a tagging structure relevant to the documents, self-study criterions and potential keywords, as well as training all members of the Self-Study Coordinating Committee (SSCC) and other selected university staff on how to enter documents into SharePoint. To deepen their understanding of the self-study, the Library Director and other self-study committee members attended the 2011 Higher Learning Commission conference.

During the second year of the self-study process SSCC criterion co-chairs, including the Library Director, continued gathering and adding evidence to SharePoint and revised drafts of their committee's self-study report. The Head of Public Services accompanied other self-study committee members to the 2012 Higher Learning Commission conference, focusing on the creation of the electronic resource room. While documents were added to the SharePoint library with a certain tagging structure and nomenclature, individuals from the SSCC would add specific self-study citations of the documents or websites which would provide evidence to their specific criterion section of the self-study text. The Head of Public Services used these citations to link evidence in the self-study report by inserting hyperlinked pdfs or websites into the text. Additionally, evidence was organized into a several indexes (Order of Appearance, Alphabetical, Subject) and a public website created for the visiting HLC team members and the Rockhurst community. This public website was called the Electronic Resource Room.[11] By the end of the process, over two thousand documents were available (figure 2.10).

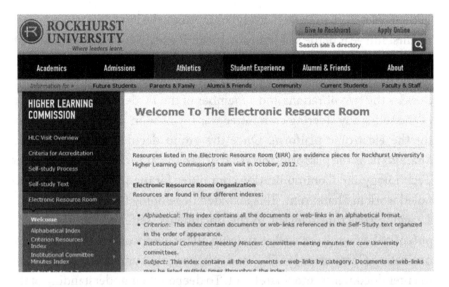

Figure 2.10. Rockhurst University Electronic Resource Room Website

Organizational changes outside the control of the library during the self-study process contributed to enhancements in their roles. Personnel changes within the technology and writing teams had a significant impact on the number of library staff involved in the final months of the self-study process. The librarians and library support staff had developed in-depth knowledge of the self-study documents and the report that was in progress. In the weeks just preceding the deadline for submission of the self-study report to the accrediting agency, the Library Director was asked by the self-study steering committee co-chairs to consider allowing these individuals to take on key roles in editing the final self-study report documents. With this deadline fast approaching and the beginning of the academic year looming, the Library Director approved the release of these library staff to accomplish the final editing of the electronic resource room, and to work with a third-party designer hired by the university to finalize the self-study report. All involved library staff had duties shifted to meet short-term needs. The self-study report and supporting documents were submitted on schedule.

As the staff prepared for the visit from the accreditation team in October, there was consistent communication between the Head of Public Services as the Chair of the Technology and Communication Team, and the chair of the site visit team. This included instruction on how to use the electronic resource room; direction to the location of specific documents; and providing additional documentation from the university if required. During the three-day site visit, the Head of Public Services, along with other university staff involved in the process, worked from the building where site visit meetings were held to provide immediate answers to team members' information requests.

The university received commendation from the visiting team for the quality of the electronic resource room and the self-study report. The Higher Learning Commission requested that the university self-study report be included in the Share Fair at the spring 2013 Higher Learning Commission Conference. In addition, in a competitive process, the Head of Public Services was selected to present a conference session on designing the electronic resource room. Both librarians were selected through peer-reviewed processes to present their experiences with the accreditation process at the 2013 Association of College and Research Libraries conference. They have also responded to requests for assistance from other institutions seeking guidance with the self-study process and organization of evidence.

Concluding Thoughts

Our essay objective is to see the roles Missouri librarians may have played in their university's self-study processes rather than to determine if the Missouri self-studies were successful. Nevertheless, we can still compare our findings to Casserly's, and note similarities and differences between our results. Many of our survey respondents mentioned that the institution received tangible benefits from the self-study process outcomes. Respondents also strongly held the belief that conducting the self-study was a way of improving the institution. One participant mentioned that the "stated shortcomings as well as advancements in different areas of the college and the library give us a more developed perspective of our situation. It motivated and made us proud." This participant felt that the internal self-study process highlighted the positives and negatives of specific university functions, and created a space for reflection and planning. Another survey participant noted that the self-study process was useful because it allowed discussion about areas that needed improvement. "[I]t was suggested that the school continue to integrate assessment processes into all of its instructional and service areas, and that improvement should be an ongoing process. However, the institution was given ten-year approval without 'concerns.'"

Role of the Academic Librarian and University Assessment

With regard to the self-study, our survey found that most librarians' were responsible for providing data. However, our experience in the accreditation process demonstrates that this role is too circumscribed. Kells emphasizes the importance of the design of the self-study process, and our experience confirms this. We assert that academic librarians should participate in the design stages of a self-study, and be represented on the accreditation self-study team. Moreover, they should be financially supported to participate in accreditation conferences, or similar professional developmental opportunities. Academic librarians should be members of the university assessment committee, and have a defined relationship with the university office of institutional effectiveness or assessment. This will facilitate the academic library's assessment of its own impact on student learning, and incorporate the unique expertise of academic librarians in gathering and organizing information. Most importantly, accrediting agencies expect the process of assessment to cross the campus community, and during accreditation, librarians' knowledge of institutional repositories and assessment systems become tremendously beneficial to the university community as a whole.

NOTES

1. B. Fister. (1998). What do they know? Assessing the Library's Contribution to Student Learning. *Library Issues* 19(1). http://homepages.gac.edu/~fister/LIassessment.html. Retrieved on March 22, 2013.
2. Greenlease Library, Rockhurst University, http://www.rockhurst.edu/library/. Retrieved on March 22, 2013.
3. Association to Advance Collegiate Schools of Business, http://www.aacsb.edu/. Retrieved on March 20, 2013.

4. Commission on Collegiate Nursing Education, http://www.aacn.nche.edu/ccne-accreditation. Retrieved on March 20, 2013.
5. These criteria were in effect at the time of the case study, but have since been updated. New criteria is available at http://www.ncahlc.org/Information-for-Institutions/criteria-and-core-components.html.
6. Higher Learning Commission "The Self-study Process in Accreditation." http://www.ncahlc.org/Self-Study/self-study-process.html
7. H.R. Kells (1995). Self-study Processes: A Guide to Self-Evaluation in Higher Education, Phoenix, AZ: Oryx Press.
8. M. Casserly (1987). Accreditation-Related Self-Study as a Planned Change Process: Factors Related to Its Success in Academic Libraries. *Journal of Academic Librarianship*, 8(1) 85-105.
9. Ibid, 95.
10. National Center for Education Statistics. Library Statistics Program: Compare Academic Libraries. http://nces.ed.gov/surveys/libraries/compare/Default.aspx. Retrieved March 22, 2013.
11. Rockhurst University Electronic Resource Room. http://www.rockhurst.edu/hlc/electronic-resource-room/welcome/ Retrieved March 21, 2013. There was also an Institutional Meeting Minutes Index of committee minutes which went back ten years. Each item in the Electronic Resource Room had a specific resource description number.

REFERENCES

Association to Advance Collegiate Schools of Business, Retrieved from http://www.aacsb.edu/ .

Casserly. M. (1987). Accreditation-Related Self-Study as a Planned Change Process: Factors Related to Its Success in Academic Libraries. *Journal of Academic Librarianship*, 8(1), 85-105.

Commission on Collegiate Nursing Education, Retrieved from http://www.aacn.nche.edu/ccne-accreditation.

Fister, Barbara. (1998. What Do They Know? Assessing the Library's Contribution to Student Learning. *Library Issues* 19(1). Retrieved from http://homepages.gac.edu/~fister/LIassessment.html.

Higher Learning Commission "The Self-study Process in Accreditation." Retrieved from http://www.ncahlc.org/Self-Study/self-study-process.html.

Kells, H. R. (1995). *Self-study Processes: A Guide to Self-Evaluation in Higher Education*, Phoenix: AZ: Oryx Press.

Rockhurst University (n.d.). Rockhurst University Electronic Resource Room. Retrieved from http://www.rockhurst.edu/hlc/electronic-resource-room/welcome/002.

Section II

Student Learning and Research

Clearing Up Mixed Messages in Library Instruction

Kacy Lundstrom
Coordinator of Library Instruction, Merrill-Cazier Library, Utah State University

Erin Davis
Library Coordinator of Regional Campuses and Distance Education, Merrill-Cazier Library, Utah State University

Introduction

Librarianship has long been interested in how to formulate messages that "stick," for populations it serves. Recent ALA President, Camila Alire, focused her term on helping librarians, at all levels, develop messages that help them become better advocates for their libraries. Marketing practices have become central themes in library literature, and in discussions about the skills that new librarians should possess. Learning to package essential information, coherently is important in nearly all areas of our profession, and academic library instruction is no exception. In fact, some discussions integral to determining best practices rely heavily on how well librarians articulate messages about what we do, the realities of the current information environment, and how students learn.

The ACRL "Standards for Proficiencies for Instruction Librarians and Co-ordinators" stress the role of communication and clarity. For example, an instruction librarian must effectively communicate with various faculty and administration to integrate information literacy (IL) standards.[1] Communication is again emphasized in standard 9.4, emphasizing the specific importance of using appropriate terminology and "avoiding excessive jargon" for various student levels.[2] These are only a few of many proficiencies that focus on the teaching librarians' role in communicating with students, instructors, coordinators and others. Laura Leavitt's discussion of skill sets required for instruction librarians in the 21st century reiterates this idea, citing "applied skills of critical thinking, collaboration, communication and creativity"[3] as essential.

Considering the continued emphasis on librarians' responsibility to clearly communicate messages, it seems that discussions about how those messages are perceived are warranted. This chapter takes a broad look at some of the overarching mixed messages librarians send to three groups: non-librarian teaching faculty, students, and amongst ourselves. We focus particularly on those messages that affect student learning.

Barbara Fister has addressed a number of these themes relating to the messages librarians are sending, and, more broadly, about instructional challenges related to communication issues. For this reason, we draw heavily upon relevant conversations in her writings. Fister and others recognize the importance of developing clarity and cohesion in our teaching. The complexities of the information landscape and the learning process, as well as the challenges to finding unity in the profession's instructional goals contribute to the "mixed" nature of our messages. Our messages are constantly in flux as evolving technology changes the way we teach, use and organize information. As we continue to evaluate and improve our messages, we will get closer to reaching our goals and strengthen our ability to facilitate real learning.

Mixed Messages with Instructors

As instruction librarians at Utah State University (USU), one of our most important responsibilities is to build collaborations with faculty that allow us to embed library instruction into the curriculum. Like so many teaching librarians, we are eager to gain entrance in the classroom, and if we are lucky, to have opportunities to shape assignments so that they meaningfully address IL.

Working with non-librarian faculty is rewarding, and challenging. Much has been published in library literature about these relationships, including issues of tenure and faculty status amongst librarians; institutional support for libraries and teaching librarians; and the feminization of the library profession and its effect on perceptions of librarians.[4] All of these issues impact the collaborations we build with faculty at our institutions.

However, other factors can impede these collaborations, including mixed messages given and received by teaching librarians and partnering faculty. One area of confusion can stem from the research assignments faculty create for their students. Occasionally librarians are given the opportunity of collaborating on the creation of the research assignment, but more often than not, the librarian collaborates with an instructor on an already prepared assignment. Consequently, the most important learning goal for the teaching librarian can get lost in the specifics of an assignment. Fister encourages librarians to think more broadly about how to tie our instruction to an entire course, beyond linking it directly to an assignment. She writes, "If you want to engage students in seeking and using information, rather than tie it to a paper, you might have students do research on the fly in ways that contribute to the course. The more impromptu and driven by curiosity these research tasks are, the more it will convey that inquiry is a normal part of everyday life."[5]

Fister emphasizes how library instruction can be integrated into a course, or even a major, reducing the resistance that students may have to library time as "busy work," and linking library work to their course and to lifelong learning. These goals go beyond simply showing tools, and providing research tips. Head and Eisenberg also allude to some of the messages instructors send regarding research through their handouts. According to their study, nearly all of the handouts collected emphasized the particulars of the assignment (page length, number of sources, etc), but neglected to inform students how to formulate a research question or strategy (2).[6] These types of handouts can send a misleading message about the most important aspects of research papers. Librarians can unwittingly support the same messages, focusing on less important matters such as mechanics and structure, rather than critical thinking and usage aspects of research.

Additionally, librarians are responsible for sending unclear messages as they market their services to instructors. When librarians approach (or are approached by) instructors for course-integrated library instruction, they often invite the instructor to bring their class to the library. This, in itself, can be a mixed message: library research and learning only happen in the library. Instructors often ask librarians to do the rote tasks they recognize that librarians do: demonstrate databases, show the library catalog, discuss the rules of the library, etc. Many librarians fail to take advantage of the opportunity to convey a larger message about IL, or about a librarian's abilities to facilitate learning activities that focus more on critical thinking, usage and evaluation throughout the research process. As Davidson, McMillen, and Maughan indicate, librarians need to work on better articulating strategies for communicating our IL goals, such as the "ACRL Information Literacy Competency Standards" to faculty: "Librarians need to be able to negotiate with faculty about the IL goals for any given assignment. Then they must be able to help tailor the assignment to better support the mutually agreed upon outcomes."[7] By increasing the awareness of IL goals on campus, we will be better positioned to advocate our goals/learning objectives more widely among the faculty we work with.

Our Response

At USU, our response has been to create instruction maps that identify classes whose curriculums best align themselves with teaching IL; we look for departmental or course learning goals that complement our IL goals. Once the most appropriate courses have been identified, librarians can work with instructors to integrate library instruction at the assignment level. This leads to fewer mixed messages amongst instructors and librarians: librarians have a clear understanding of the instructor's goals for assignments, and for the course. And this clarity provides the librarian with opportunities to articulate and integrate lesson plans that lead to real learning in the areas students need it most.

We have also found it helpful to join instructors in their classroom the day the assignment is introduced. This enables us to be even more aware of the messages instructors are sending students, and how we, as librarians, can work within the assignment structure to help students succeed. Also, if we are more familiar with the assignment and the teacher's learning goals, we are more able to integrate instruction that focuses on larger goals instead of solely focusing on the particulars of an assignment (i.e. finding five scholarly articles on a topic vs. learning real-life principles of credibility and researched support). Finally, we try to limit the odds for students to feel they are receiving conflicting messages from the library and their instructor.

In order to accommodate library sessions that address learning goals relating to evaluation and usage, we started moving basic skill instruction to online forums, creating videos and tutorials that can be embedded in library guides or into a learning management system. We recognize that many students still need to know basic pieces of information, such as "where is the full text of this article?", "what is a database?" and "how do I search the library catalog?" to name a few of many introductory questions. However, considering the preciousness of in-person library instruction, moving much of the demonstration information to video is a viable way to free up class time. Jeremy Donald suggests a similar model that enables librarians to promote authentic student learning by spending more valuable in-class time on higher-level concepts, such as critical thinking.[8] Shifting from the more traditional lecture-based models to concept-based teaching allows us to help students understand IL in more demanding and practical contexts.

Mixed Messages with Students

Message reception is particularly complicated among students, mostly because they come from such varied backgrounds and have different expertise levels. Clearly communicating with students can also be difficult because we send countless messages to students about our roles as librarians; the research process; and the "right" way to do a range of research-related tasks.

Leading students through the nuances of research is laden with landmines. Some students understand what the message "be selective with Google" means; others will interpret that as meaning "Google is bad." These sorts of didactic messages, whether intentionally or unintentionally sent, are misleading, and can lead to a lot of false assumptions. Because Google links directly to many library collections, making generalizations, without allowing for critical thinking regarding use and purpose, can be confusing for students. We are inadvertently sending students mixed messages by making broad statements about the search tools they have come to rely on. Fister agrees that we are taking it too easy on students by sending these types of superficial messages: "we are not really teaching students to think, we are teaching them to judge books by their covers."[9] As librarians, we tend to make blanket statements about the dangers of using Wikipedia and Google, but we often fail to discuss today's information landscape in practical, honest ways.

Librarians also send mixed messages to students each time we instruct them on finding information for a research paper. Many of us fail to communicate the larger purpose of a research paper in an undergraduate career, and lose opportunities to engage students in conversations about where information comes from, and why it matters. Failing to communicate the purpose of an assignment or lesson can often cause students to feel disinterested. Communicating this is not the only issue—the debate continues over the intended purpose of these assignments. Fister enters this debate, speculating whether it is more important to teach students about tools of the discipline, or help them form research questions and building evidence-based arguments.[10] These varied purposes, while not antithetical, can be confusing to students, especially if librarians and instructors are not united in their answer.

Mixed messages are amplified by students' perceptions regarding their own research skills. Students come to the classroom with preconceived notions about how research works—because it has worked for them in the past—and many feel they already possess the skills they need to conduct research successfully. Becker points out "computer literacy does not naturally equate to information literacy."[11] While it is important to recognize the technological and information seeking skills many students possess, these same skills can be less relevant in the context of library materials. And, while many students use Google frequently, the process is often hindered by the same barriers they encounter in library databases: a lack of understanding of how search engines work, and a lack of evaluation.

There are other contradictions in students' experiences with "successful" research, and many face difficulties when they switch from using old methods—such as Google—to library resources, including databases that produce vastly different results and require new techniques. Librarians' inability to make the connection between the landscape students recognize and the library information landscape can cause students to negatively perceive library information as unattainable or difficult to find. Interpreting and navigating vast library resources can be daunting prospect for a student researcher, especially since many of our databases are poorly designed. According to Alan Jacobs, "…there's one vital issue [librarians are] neglecting: research databases have the worst user interfaces *in the whole world*."[12] Librarians may assure students that library databases will produce better results, but when this does not occur, either because of search strategies or simply because databases do not contain the desired information, students are less willing to listen to other messages from librarians, including those that address the nuances and complications of using library databases.

The language students, instructors, and librarians employ when discussing research is also implicated in mixed messages. Holliday and Rogers discuss the importance of using language that emphasizes learning from information, rather than finding sources. "Finding sources" is often the service that librarians are associated with; this is a message sent by instructors, librarians and students. They write, "we are now highly conscious of the limiting nature of 'finding sources' and the need to shift our discourse and activities towards 'learning more about.'"[13] The shift in terminology is evidence of a shift in pedagogy. Research is not about simply finding a pile of information—plenty of students have proven they can do this easily. It is more difficult, and integral to the research process, to learn how to "learn more about" something, which follows naturally from reading and synthesizing information, rather than just collecting it.

Our Response

During our instruction sessions, we try to first establish that we recognize the information landscape students come from. Questions like, "Where do you start when you do not know anything?," usually leads to important conversations about how and when to use Google and Wikipedia. Students still expect to be given checklist type messages like "do not use Wikipedia," so beginning a session by acknowledging that there are legitimate uses for the resources they are comfortable with is a good way to get students thinking about usage and purpose, and to validate what students' knowledge and experience.

Asking students for their definition of "research" is another good segue into the conversation about a research paper's purpose. This can lead to discussions about where to find information, and why evaluation of sources matters. USU librarians have incorporated active learning strategies to help students recognize the role of inquiry in research. We have even experimented with having students investigate academic or professional discourse communities to expose them to the ways different disciplines communicate information.

We also encourage students to spend the library instruction session with one goal: to find one resource that can inform their understanding of their topic. Students usually welcome the opportunity to have free printing in our instruction rooms, but printing off twelve articles that may or may not be useful to them does not make their research process easier. Fister writes, "for librarians, the implications are rather more stark. We tend to think more is always better, that helping students do research means exposing them to a huge banquet of options."[14] Instead, we encourage students to be discerning with their time and their research by encouraging them to find one good thing that interests them and furthers their understanding of the topic, students have a workable goal for that library session. Their research becomes more deliberate. The objective is to allow for actual reading and synthesis of information to take place, which often becomes clouded by emphasis on finding and searching.

Once students have begun to read relevant research that informs their topic, we spend the consecutive instruction session encouraging them to use that information to find more related information. It is a simple notion, but one that is a foreign idea to students who are used to simply clicking from a list of Google results, or even results from a scholarly database. Focusing on how resources "converse" with other resources emphasizes scholarly discourse, rather than the source itself. It also takes the emphasis off the database. It does not pit Google against library databases; it simply encourages students to connect information together, wherever it exists. This leads to a better understanding of a topic, and to a stronger likelihood that students will develop and use their own voice to enter a conversation, rather than simply reiterating what they found in their sources.

Although we haven't addressed all the mixed messages we send to students, by constantly assessing our classroom efforts we can continue to respond to these problems with practical solutions.

Mixed Messages among Librarians

As librarians, our primary goal is to help students become critical thinkers, and ultimately lifelong learners. But as we traverse the changing information landscape, this can feel like a daunting task, especially when the profession sends conflicting messages about what we are trying to achieve. The literature is ripe with opinions on how to best spend the time we get with students, especially when that time is allocated in 50-minute segments once or twice a semester.[15] Because we have so much material to cover, many of us resort to "canned database lectures" rather than designing lesson plans tailored to the class's learning objectives. Yet teaching librarians must rethink and reevaluate our educational mission so we can help students understand research in more challenging and practical contexts.

Deciding which IL skills to emphasize can be difficult when planning a library instruction session. There is an ongoing debate about which learning goals should be included typical library instruction session, and about who should teach specific objectives. Some believe the librarian should teach basic research skills to students, and disciplinary tools/concepts for upper-divisional classes should be taught by faculty.[16] Others believe we are doing a disservice to the profession by focusing so heavily on generic IL skills, and insist we must push for a more "comprehensive view of information literacy in higher education."[17]

It is also challenging for librarians to strike the right balance of how much information to provide during library instruction sessions and research consultations. Our instinct is to turn students into what Fister calls "mini-librarians," instead of equipping them with higher-level critical thinking skills. She writes, "there is no reason that we have to teach navigating the library, evaluation of sources, close reading, organizing ideas in written form, citation rules, *and* how and whether to summarize, paraphrase, or quote directly from sources all in a single, high-stakes assignment."[18] Attempting to cram all of those goals into one, two, or even three sessions is difficult and often deteriorates into quick "show and tell" methods, and can create mixed messages. Many library instructors fail to rely on learning activities that teach difficult concepts like synthesis and evaluation for usage, perhaps because these lesson plans take more time and skill. It can be challenging to veer from traditional formats like demonstrating and lecturing to promote authentic student learning, especially since most librarians lack formal teaching backgrounds.

Librarians also generate mixed messages about how to define our information literacy goals. In this way, complete reliance on the ACRL Standards to measure how effectively we are teaching can be problematic. Although the standards provide an important benchmark to ensure librarians teach the same concepts, they tend to emphasize discrete skills. It can be unrealistic to design our teaching around these goals, particularly if we want to broaden the scope of IL in the academy.[19] And simply relying on these standards to communicate our messages about what IL is, and what role it should play in our classrooms and on our campuses, is not sufficient.

The lack of unity in the profession about how to define, teach, and explain information literacy directly affects our ability to leverage crucial support from faculty and administration. To ensure that IL instruction is woven throughout the curriculum, we need to work on conveying the importance of IL within our academic communities. However, many librarians have not developed strong negotiating strategies to communicate IL's relevance and importance, sometimes because we are uncertain about IL best practices. This means faculty and administration are not familiar with the learning objectives, assessment strategies, and pedagogies we believe should be included in most IL courses.[20] As we bring more clarity and cohesion to the messages our profession transmits, gaining buy-in for IL programs and reforms from our institutions will become easier.

Our Response

At USU, we have a highly course-integrated IL program and strong relationships with many of our departments. We have largely stopped doing long demonstrations, and instead incorporate active learning techniques into each session, which stress critical thinking skills. We are able to do this by cultivating relationships with each faculty member we work with, and making the time to have conversations about their learning goals for each session, while also articulating our own objectives. We have also embedded ourselves programmatically wherever possible. For example, in the writing department, we collaborate on the first-year composition curriculum. The integration of a librarian into every section of first -and second-year composition classes is heavily supported by the Director of the Writing Program. When IL strategies need to be revised or clarified (based on formal and informal assessments), sharing our data and observations with the director helps us garner support from the writing instructors we work with. Having his buy-in first, and having him share our goals, allows us to present a more cohesive message to writing instructors, and allows greater potential for real change. Open lines of communication with administration, and carefully honed messages supported by shared research and assessment, allows us to have a stronger instructional impact . As we attempt to articulate a broader vision of IL, this close collaboration reduces mixed messages between faculty and administration.

When conducting a session, we have found that selecting one or two ACRL Information Literacy Standards most relevant to a class assignment is more manageable than attempting to "cover everything." According to the Project Information Literacy survey, students already know how to find information, and other surface-learning activities,[21] so we have refocused our instruction efforts to Standard 4, which states "the information literate student, individually or as a member of a group, uses information effectively to accomplish a specific purpose."[22] Students tend to struggle most with synthesis and integration of sources, so to use our limited time most efficiently, we try to focus on this standard, rather than demonstrating a database. Teaching students how to use and evaluate information is difficult; we are constantly attempting new learning activities to more closely focus on research strategies/tactics/elements that students struggle with the most. Despite the difficulties, we continue to try to gear our instruction efforts in that direction.

In an attempt to make our library collections more user-friendly and reduce our mixed messages to novice researchers, we redesigned the library website with the end user in mind. Many librarians fail to design their collections with novice researchers in mind, and instead add to their collections each year, making the database list more unwieldy, and overwhelming students even more. Librarians tend to err on the side of providing too much information instead of arming students with strategies to find the best resources for their paper. As Fister points out, "the means undergraduates have developed of reducing the aperture, of focusing their attention to a manageable set of options, is a survival strategy that we should consider as we design library collections..."[23]

Although we want to help students at with their immediate needs, sometimes our efforts can backfire when we give students too much information, particularly when they are still grappling with the whole idea of a research paper and still learning about their topic. Promoting discovery tools is one approach that gives novice researchers a more manageable set of options to work with. Situated prominently on the USU library's front page is the discovery layer, "Summon," allows students to search books and articles simultaneously. Librarians at USU have encouraged students to begin their search process there, in the hope that students will get a cursory but helpful look at information written on a particular topic. We hope to minimize students' confusion, and to give them a single point of entry for their research.

All of these responses represent our attempts to address some of the controversies within the librarian community, and to become more unified in how we have decided to address them at our university.

Conclusion

The organizational culture at USU's Merrill-Cazier Library encourages constant experimentation with best practices. As teaching librarians, we endeavor to implement and experiment with ideas that focus on student-centered active learning. Nearly all of these attempts require close collaboration with faculty, and with librarians willing to do more than demonstrate a database.

Most of our responses, as described in this chapter, are attempts at clarifying best practices for garnering support for embedded librarianship, and for spending class time in ways that meet the most important learning goals. These goals are impacted by all three groups discussed above, and integral to so many discussions occurring in library instruction.

We certainly do not claim to have resolved all the mixed messages between instructors and the embedded librarians they work with, between students and librarians, and between librarians within our own profession. Such conversations are ongoing, and essential to continuous improvement and growth in these areas. We focus broadly on a number of mixed messages relating to library instruction, but further research and expansion is needed in each of these areas.

By examining our behaviors and our verbal messages closely, we can determine if we are sending accurate messages that articulate our most important goals—those that lead to authentic student learning. If we communicate our higher learning goals without clearly conveying where and how IL should be woven into the curriculum, it is likely that we will continue to perpetuate the stereotype that librarians are the "gatekeepers of information." Those outside of the profession will continue to see us as people who only peripherally show their students library resources, and not as professionals who can help students and faculty with the complexities of the research process. By being clear and reflective about the messages we send and how they are being perceived, we will be better prepared to serve our institutions and to further our impact in the area of library instruction.

NOTES

1. Association of College and Research Libraries, "Standards for Proficiencies for Instruction Librarians and Coordinators: A Practical Guide," *Association of College and Research Libraries, A division of the American Library Association,* Chicago: Association of College and Research Libraries, American Library Association, 2008: 571.
2. Ibid., p. 574.
3. Leavitt, Laura. "21st Century Workforce Initiatives: Implications for Information Literacy Instruction in Academic Libraries." *Education Libraries* 34, no. 2 (2011): 15-18.
4. Golub, Erin Marie. "Gender Divide in Librarianship: Past, Present, and Future." *Library Student Journal* 5, no. 7 (2010); Gillum, Shalu. "The True Benefit of Faculty Status for Academic Reference Librarians." *Reference Librarian* 51, no. 4 (October 2010): 321-328; Hill, Janet Swan. "Constant Vigilance, Babelfish, and Foot Surgery: Perspectives on Faculty Status and Tenure for Academic Librarians." *Portal: Libraries & The Academy* 5, no. 1 (January 2005): 7-22.
5. Fister, Barbara, "Resisting the Robo-Assignment," *Library Babel Fish* (blog), May 2, 2012,

http://www.insidehighered.com/blogs/library-babel-fish/resisting-robo-assignment.

6. Head, Alison J. and Michael B. Eisenberg. "Assigning Inquiry: How Handouts for Research Assignments Guide Today's College Students," *Project Information Literacy Progress Report*, University of Washington's Information School, July 12, 2010.

7. Davidson, Jeanne R., Paula S. McMillen, and Laurel S. Maughan. "Using the 'ACRL Information Literacy Competency Standards for Higher Education' to Assess a University Library Instruction Program." *Journal of Library Administration* 36, no. 1-2 (2002): 97-121.

8. Donald, Jeremy, "Using Technology to Support Faculty and Enhance Coursework at Academic Institutions." *Texas Library Journal* 85, no. 4 (2010): 129-131.

9. Fister, Barbara, "Teaching How Information Works, Not How to Work Information," *Library Journal* Peer-to-Peer Review (blog), March 1, 2012, http://lj.libraryjournal. com/2012/03/opinion/peer-to-peer-review/teaching-how-information-works-not-how-to-work-information-peer-to-peer-review/.

10. ———."Undergraduates in the Library Trying Not to Drown," *Library Babel Fish* (blog), November 1, 2010, http://www.insidehighered.com/blogs/library_babel_fish/undergraduates_in_the_library_trying_not_to_drown.

11. Becker, Charles H. "Student Values and Research: Are Millennials Really Changing the Future of Reference and Research?" *Journal of Library Administration*, 49 no. 4 (2009): 342.

12. Jacobs, Alan. "Google Trained Minds Can't Deal With Terrible Research Database UI." *The Atlantic Monthly*, 309 no. 3 (Feb. 27, 2012).

13. Holliday, Wendy and Jim Rogers. "Talking About Information Literacy: The Mediating Role of Discourse in a College Writing Classroom." Unpublished manuscript, 2012, p. 27.

14. Fister, Barbara. "Undergraduates in the Library Trying Not to Drown," *Library Babel Fish* (blog), November 1, 2010, http://www.insidehighered.com/blogs/library_babel_fish/undergraduates_in_the_library_trying_not_to_drown.

15. Lorenzen, Michael. "Active Learning and Library Instruction." *Illinois Libraries*, 83 no. 2 (2001): 19-24.

16. Grafstein, Ann. "A Discipline-Based Approach to Information Literacy." *Journal of Academic Librarianship* 28, no. 4 (2002): 197-204.

17. Owusu-Ansah, Edward K. "Information Literacy and Higher Education: Placing the Academic Library in the Center of a Comprehensive Solution." *Journal of Academic Librarianship* 30, no. 1 (2004): 3.

18. Fister, Barbara, "Resisting the Robo-Assignment," *Library Babel Fish* (blog), May 2, 2012, http://www.insidehighered.com/blogs/library-babel-fish/resisting-robo-assignment.

19. Johnston, Bill and Sheila Webber, "Information Literacy in Higher Education: A Review and Case Study." *Studies in Higher Education* 28 no. 3 (2003): 335-352; Owusu-Ansah, Edward K. "Information Literacy and the Academic Library: A Critical Look at a Concept and the Controversies Surrounding It." *Journal of Academic Librarianship* 29 no. 4 (2003): 219-230.

20. Macklin PhD, Alexius Smith and F. Bartow Culp PhD, "Information Literacy Instruction: Competencies, Caveats, and a Call to Action." *Science & Technology Libraries* 28 no. 1-2 (2008): 49.

21. Head, Alison J. and Michael B. Eisenberg. "Truth Be Told: How College Students Evaluate and Use Information in the Digital Age." *Project Information Literacy Progress Report*, University of Washington's Information School, November 1, 2010.

22. ACRL. "Information Literacy Competency Standards for Higher Education." American Library Association, January 18, 2000, http://www.ala.org/acrl/standards/informationliteracycompetency.

23. Fister, Barbara. "Undergraduates in the Library Trying Not to Drown," *Library Babel Fish* (blog), November 1, 2010, http://www.insidehighered.com/blogs/library_babel_fish/undergraduates_in_the_library_trying_not_to_drown.

REFERENCES

ACRL, American Library Association (2000). *Information Literacy Competency Standards for Higher Education.* Retrieved from http://www.ala.org/acrl/standards/informationliteracy-competency.

Association of College and Research Libraries, American Library Association (2008). *Standards for Proficiencies for Instruction Librarians and Coordinators: A Practical Guide.* Chicago: Association of College and Research Libraries.

Becker, C. H., (2009). Student Values and Research: Are Millennials Really Changing the Future of Reference and Research? *Journal of Library Administration, 49*(4), 342.

Davidson, J. R., McMillen, P. S., and Maughan L. S., (2002). Using the 'ACRL Information Literacy Competency Standards for Higher Education' to Assess a University Library Instruction Program. *Journal of Library Administration, 36*(1-2), 97-121.

Donald, J., (2010). Using Technology to Support Faculty and Enhance Coursework at Academic Institutions. *Texas Library Journal, 85*(4), 129-131.

Fister, B., (2012, March 1). Teaching How Information Works, Not How to Work Information [Web log comment]. Retrieved from http://lj.libraryjournal.com/2012/03/opinion/peer-to-peer-review/teaching-how-information-works-not-how-to-work-information-peer-to-peer-review/.

Fister, B., (2012, May 2). Resisting the Robo-Assignment [Web log comment]. Retrieved from http://www.insidehighered.com/blogs/library-babel-fish/resisting-robo-assignment.

Fister, B., (2010, November 1). Undergraduates in the Library Trying Not to Drown [Web log comment]. Retrieved from http://www.insidehighered.com/blogs/library_babel_fish/undergraduates_in_the_library_trying_not_to_drown.

Gillum, S., (2010). The True Benefit of Faculty Status for Academic Reference Librarians. *Reference Librarian, 51*(4), 321-328.

Golub, E. M., (2010). Gender Divide in Librarianship: Past, Present, and Future. *Library Student Journal, 5*(7).

Grafstein, A., (2002). A Discipline-Based Approach to Information Literacy. *Journal of Academic Librarianship, 28*(4), 197-204.

Head, A. J., and Eisenberg. M. B., (2010). Assigning Inquiry: How Handouts for Research Assignments Guide Today's College Students. *Project Information Literacy Progress Report, University of Washington's Information School.*

Head, A. J., and Eisenberg. M. B., (2010). Truth Be Told: How College Students Evaluate and Use Information in the Digital Age. *Project Information Literacy Progress Report, University of Washington's Information School.*

Hill, J. S., (2005). Constant Vigilance, Babelfish, and Foot Surgery: Perspectives on Faculty Status and Tenure for Academic Librarians. *Portal: Libraries & The Academy, 5*(1), 7-22.

Holliday, W. and Rogers J., (2012). *Talking About Information Literacy: The Mediating Role of Discourse in a College Writing Classroom.* Unpublished manuscript.

Jacobs, A., (2012). Google Trained Minds Can't Deal With Terrible Research Database UI. *The Atlantic Monthly, 309*(3).

Johnston, B. and Webber S., (2003). Information Literacy in Higher Education: A Review and Case Study. *Studies in Higher Education, 28*(3), 335-352

Leavitt, L., (2011). 21st Century Workforce Initiatives: Implications for Information Literacy Instruction in Academic Libraries. *Educational Libraries, 34*(2), 15-18.

Lorenzen, M., (2001). Active Learning and Library Instruction. *Illinois Libraries, 83*(2), 19-24.

Macklin A. S., and Culp F. B., (2008). Information Literacy Instruction: Competencies, Caveats, and a Call to Action. *Science & Technology Libraries, 28*(1-2), 49.

Owusu-Ansah, E. K. (2003). Information Literacy and the Academic Library: A Critical Look at a Concept and the Controversies Surrounding It. *Journal of Academic Librarianship, 29*(4), 219-230.

Owusu-Ansah, E. K., (2004). Information Literacy and Higher Education: Placing the Academic Library in the Center of a Comprehensive Solution. *Journal of Academic Librarianship, 30*(1), 3.

Wong, P., Todaro, J., (2010). Frontline Advocacy is Everybody's Job. *American Libraries, 41*(6-7), 82-84.

Swimming in the Matrix:
A Dialogue on Teaching Undergraduate Research

Iris Jastram
Reference and Instruction Librarian, Laurence McKinley Gould Library, Carleton College

Steve Lawson
Humanities Librarian, Tutt Library, Colorado College

As instruction librarians at small liberal arts colleges—and therefore as two librarians in jobs very similar to Barbara Fister's—we have learned a great deal from and with Barbara over the years. Her writing and her conversations often reveal fully articulated versions of ideas that we have just begun forming ourselves, which is validating and humbling. But even more than that, her deep and fundamental respect for undergraduates and their learning process, combined with her ability to speak out forcefully and constructively, have put her in the position of being an informal mentor for so many of us who "want to be Barbara when we grow up."

One key theme woven throughout Barbara's work is the importance of finding and having a voice, and of honoring the voices of others. For undergraduates, this means finding their own voices while also incorporating the voices of others into their ever more robust knowledge constructs. They cannot download knowledge from one brain to another, but they can engage with ideas and use that engagement to foster knowledge building.

The same is true of other learners. Even librarians!

Like undergraduates, librarians, also learn by engaging with ideas, either through direct conversation or through the drawn-out conversations between articles and blog posts and conference presentations. What follows is just such a conversation. Each of us will present our individual ideas on how instruction librarians can work most meaningfully with undergraduate researchers, and then we will engage in a dialogue about those ideas, helping each other clarify and expand our understandings of the topic. Ultimately, we hope to come to a deeper understanding of our fundamental goals as instruction librarians, share a few ideas about how to translate those goals to the classroom, and do it all in a way that celebrates Barbara's conviction that knowledge is born of engaged interaction.

Iris on Undergraduate Research: This isn't Stamp Collecting!

Librarians and undergrads have one thing in common: we are obsessed with the "finding things" definition of research. When I was in library school, everything—from designing databases to bibliometrics to cataloging—had "finding things" as its driving motivation. Ask anyone what a librarian does and we are likely to say some variation on "find things."

Meanwhile, undergrads are similarly primed for focusing myopically on finding things whenever research projects appear on the syllabus. They want a couple of sources that back up their thoughts, point-by-point, and they want one hopelessly laughable source that can serve simultaneously as counterargument and whipping boy. As students see it, their job is to gather together something akin to a brief on the topic of choice: patch together the useful parts of the good sources; flay the bad source alive; and arrive at what John Bean calls an "all about" paper[1] designed to show a professor that the student is capable of informing a hypothetical reader "all about" the important things to know about a topic. In an ongoing research project I am part of, the Information Literacy in Student Writing (ILSW) project, this shallow understanding of research shows up all over the place in the form of "patch writing"[2] and over-citation.[3] "See?" says the student through the wide margins next to block quotes, "I did it! I found out everything you need to know about global warming and condensed it for you into a digestible five-page essay!"

So here we all are, pulling for the same goal, over and over, and constantly disappointed with the results. Librarians train students in the fine art of finding things, students are bored but find things anyway, librarians feel undervalued, classroom faculty are underwhelmed, and our ILSW project keeps revealing patch-written "all about" papers. Maybe our goals need to be adjusted.

"But finding things is what we do," some librarians might say. "If we adjust that goal, are we not becoming something else?" Not at all. "Use information effectively" is one of the ACRL Information Literacy Standards,[4] so there is nothing in our Information Literacy contract that forces us to draw the boundaries of our expertise well within the "finding things" part of research. In fact, doing so may actually be a disservice for our students.

Of course, this doesn't mean that we should all go become writing instructors. Imagine, though, the impact of teaching *parallel* to disciplinary faculty, rather than off in a *cul de sac* on the side. All of a sudden, the disciplinary faculty and librarians become tracks the students can trolley along, each reinforcing the other, and each track guiding students toward more effective work. And, as Barbara Fister has pointed out over and over again, librarians can fulfill their part of the bargain relatively easily by remembering and making explicit that research is part of a fundamentally rhetorical act. As she says, "Rather than describe the search process as a matter of finding information—which sounds like panning for solid nuggets of truth—librarians should describe it as a way of tapping into a scholarly communication network."[5] And later, "Placing research skills in a rhetorical framework will make the search process more meaningful and the evaluation of sources more natural for students. And more important, it will help students to situate their research findings in a text of their own that uses evidence in a more sophisticated and successful way."[6] The emphasis, then, is on the connections between ideas and the conversations that these connections enact. It is not all about "finding things." It is about igniting students' imaginations. It is about revealing how students can engage with outside knowledge to build their own well-grounded ideas and to communicate those ideas effectively.

Steve on Undergraduate Research: From Curators to Creators

I often find library instruction unsatisfying. My complaints are familiar: my time with the class is too brief, my relationship with the students too tenuous, my lesson too isolated from the rest of the course. But, like all academic instruction librarians, I am hopeful and diligent, and with each class I teach, I look at the students' research assignment and try to carve out a piece of that project to call my own. In the past, this piece almost always amounted to searching for sources in library-approved databases and full-text collections.

But when I taught that way, when I pulled out "searching for sources" as my sole contribution to a class I got to see once for an hour or so, I found that I was reinforcing a problematic attitude toward research. Students would speak of their research paper as if the "research" was something wholly different and divorced from the "paper." Like tying your shoes before you play basketball, or putting gas in the tank before going for a drive, students seemed to know that research was necessary, but also seemed to expect it to be quick, preliminary, and mostly a technical barrier to the real work of writing. When I got in front of them and pulled out canned searches of my own devising to demonstrate the features of the article database, I was reinforcing this view of research as a technical or even bureaucratic skill. I was reinforcing a way of researching and writing that too often ends up with students writing generally about a topic, rather than creating and supporting a compelling argument.

I suspected there was something more, an approach perhaps implied by the multi-faceted ACRL Information Literacy Standards,[7] but not fully articulated there as a pedagogy. I was attracted to the writing center on our campus, where it seemed to me that student tutors and clients alike took their writing far more seriously than their research. I wondered, what, if anything, could make those students as engaged with research as they were with writing: how could research feel as personal, as necessary, as high-stakes as writing did? I began to change the way I taught from being a "specialist" who passed on highly specific tips about this or that library database, to being more of a coach or even a counselor. I tried to first draw the class out with questions about their work and their ideas, and only once I'd established this context—this *need* for sources or evidence—would I turn on the classroom projector and start talking about searching.

Whenever I have a good idea about teaching and learning in libraries, I always find out that Barbara Fister has beaten me to it. Sometimes she's only ahead of me by a few days, posting a fully developed column online while I am still mulling over the implications. But just as often—as in this case—it turns out that Barbara is a decade or more ahead of me. In 1990, or about twenty years before I started thinking about this problem in earnest, Barbara wrote about how students are too likely to see themselves as "hunters and gatherers" who use sources simply as collections of facts which they report back on in their papers.[8] Librarians are not the only source or cause of the students' misconceptions, of course, but through our teaching we can help students develop a view of themselves as creators of knowledge, and less as collectors and curators of knowledge. If we're successful, knowledge "is not something that grows by accretion of new discoveries (that can be written up, set on the library shelf and located whenever a dose of truth is required), but changes depending on the way in which the interpreting community views it."[9]

After more than twenty years, I would have hoped that our profession would have better internalized and formalized this understanding of how we should address teaching research skills. And perhaps with ACRL's Information Literacy Immersion program, we are getting there. But it still seems like this integrated view of research, rhetoric, and writing is something that we need to relearn and reteach with some regularity. I am heartened somewhat by the fact that Fister herself is still returning to this subject, finding new insights and new metaphors. In the winter of 2012 Fister wrote: "We need to help students understand the vast web of meaning in the making and develop ways to shape their own ideas about what parts to pay attention to. They need to know not just how to find finished information but how to grasp meaning as it's made and how to participate in its making. ... I had a frustrating time this week helping students explore databases, which seem like supremely clumsy boutique shopping sites for products that are each sold separately, detached from the network that produced them."[10]

Instruction librarians are not personal shoppers, we are consumer advocates. By the time I have added this idea to my repertoire, I am sure Barbara Fister will have long moved on to another idea that I'll think of later.

Dialogic Learning: Iris and Steve Discuss Undergraduate Research

Iris: I find it really interesting that when we each articulated what we saw as the deep underlying problem in the way that undergraduates understand research (and therefore in the ways that we see our jobs), I talked about how undergraduates misunderstand the point of gathering information, while you talked about how the major problem is that undergraduates see information gathering as distinct and separate from writing.

I wonder if these conclusions point to the *same* deep underlying problem, or if you think they are two problems that often happen together.

Steve: I think that research and writing is problematic overall, I guess. It is full of problems, and part of the process is understanding or overcoming those problems or making those problems work for you.

Even in the short time since I wrote my contribution at the start of this chapter, I have been thinking about how students see that split between researching and writing. And I think what they actually do is more complicated than research first, writing later. In fact, the work that Barbara did in the 1990s shortly after the article that I quoted pointed to undergraduates having more complicated and recursive methods than perhaps I gave them credit for.[11]

I should also say that I don't think it is crazy for them to want to do the research first, because they are so often working from a state of near-total ignorance.

Iris: Yes, that is true.

Steve: Before they can even articulate a question, they have a lot of reading to do. I think part of it might be a vocabulary problem, as in, they refer to all this initial reading as "research." And then if they have time, or are diligent enough, they actually do continue to read even as they write and revise. But they don't necessarily think of that as "research," they think of it as "writing."

Iris: Ahh, that makes a lot of sense to me because it *is* research, but not done for the same purpose.
On top of all of this, undergraduates are making a difficult transition, I think, from school to higher education—from learning about things to learning to actually produce new knowledge based on all that background they finally know. I think they are often not yet used to their goal being to create knowledge.

Steve: Yes, and I sometimes see terrible confusion about the role of "opinion" in student writing. Some students have been told that papers shouldn't be their opinion, so they are very careful to say nothing controversial or original. Or interesting. Then their college professor says, "I need you to write more about what you think of the subject," and they feel stuck between two poles.

Iris: Right. "Opinion" is kind of like "research" in that we (and classroom faculty) use them to mean "independent thought" and "discovery and synthesis" while students think they mean "feelings"
and "background." And all of this gets compounded by misunderstandings about where knowledge-creation actually happens.
Students think "over there, with the experts" and we are trying to
tell them, "No, in *you*—in your head, where you synthesize all this
stuff from other people."

Steve: Yes, and in fact, in one of these articles Barbara says that we
should teach constructivist knowledge creation by example—giving students a chance to see how we create knowledge in our own
heads.[12] Is that something that you try to do in the classroom?

Iris: I must, because that is how I think learning happens, but I wonder
what examples I actually set that help students learn to recognize
it for themselves. What do you do?

Steve: I have never, until this moment, sat down and thought, "how do I
teach constructivist knowledge creation by example?" But I think
that I do by exposing my ignorance to the classes I talk to. I try
and let them know when I don't know what I am talking about.
I don't use canned searches very often, and instead try and work
with what the students are actually interested in and what they
have told me in that moment. For example, I will point out that I
am doing a really dumb search with just one keyword from them
and I am expecting to get back lots of weird results.

And then I talk through how I look at the results and use them to
teach myself something about the topic — what kinds of journals
are publishing on the topic, what kinds of confusion or false hits I
can expect, and so on. So I am starting from a position of ignorance, but learning through the research process.

I think that might be what Barbara is talking about, if on a pretty basic level. I am using the act of research to create a basic level of knowledge as I work. Then I also talk about why certain things we find in the results might be interesting, and that is very rarely because "it will probably have facts I need."

I notice as I tell you this, though, that I am still pretty well stuck in the "finding things" model that you say we need to get beyond.

Iris: Well, I think we can never get rid of that entirely. That would be throwing out babies with bath water. I think that there are probably lots of places to work in examples of and practice with knowledge creation, and certainly doing so while finding things is important too.

You have made me think about my earlier statement that I am not aware having the goal of teaching constructivist knowledge creation by example, but I *am* aware that I have shifted my conception of my underlying goal from "help them find things" to "show them The Matrix." So when I teach about attribution and bibliographies, for example, I teach them more about academic sociology than about citation styles.

I want them to see each piece of information not as a golden "nugget of truth"[13] but as a node, almost. As a place that connects to a whole bunch of other people and ideas and articulations.

I want them to take the red pill.

Steve: I think that is a very valuable approach. In some cases you will be reinforcing what the professors are already teaching them about the discipline, but in many cases it seems like the professors are fish and the academic discipline is the water. You are throwing the students a snorkel.

Iris: And fins! Because the student has to get up to speed pretty quickly.

Steve: Right, yes. Swimming in the Matrix.

Iris: You can't have too many metaphors

Steve: Metaphors are the sand on the beach. *Anyway*... I was thinking of the way you ended your piece. "It is not all about finding things. It is about igniting students' imaginations..." And while I do not disagree, I was wondering about the student who just is not catching fire.

The great Russian director Stanislavski wrote about how an actor cannot expect to be "inspired" on command, that inspiration comes rarely and technique has to carry the load a lot of the time. So can we teach students about doing research when they are not really inspired or on fire, when they are merely on deadline?

Iris: Well, I do not think that the "here is how you" approach to teaching will help either the inspired or the uninspired.

Steve: Yes, very good point!

Iris: If we think of our one session as one experience in a while long set of experiences in which students develop good information literate habits of mind, then even if your one session does not make a huge impression, at least it is not digging the student deeper into misconceptions about the nature and purpose of research. So I try not to teach things very differently, though I certainly do have to work harder to engage some classes, for sure. And some classes do not turn out well.

And just now, as we are talking, I realize that all of this is modeling knowledge creation! I was doing it all along!

Steve: And simultaneously speaking prose!

Iris: Amazing!

Steve: I think I understand what you are saying, and I certainly do not think that the best way to reach bored uninspired students is to be boring and uninspired ourselves.

I think I am just hoping to abstract this a bit more, so that I can tell students explicitly or implicitly, "here are techniques that will help take you from choosing a subject through to a finished paper, and they will help you regardless of how excited and intellectually engaged you are."

I think that is one appeal of teaching "finding stuff." Finding stuff will never let you down. You can assess finding stuff. Did they find stuff? Excellent, assessment complete. It is a lot more difficult to assess an imagination on fire.

Iris: Yes, I think that is true. And that is why I have resisted many of the more simplistic assessment efforts floating around, not wanting to be even further reduced to that function just for the sake of numbers. But going back to your example from acting, I wonder what an acting coach would be able to teach us about reaching the uninspired. You talked in your essay about moving from being a "specialist" to being a "coach or even a counselor." I wonder how an acting coach would approach the problem.

Steve: One thing that actors have to do is put themselves in other people's shoes and see things from that person or character's point of view. It is pointless for an actress to say, "well, I am just not that ambitious" if she's playing Lady Macbeth.

Iris: Several of Lady Macbeth's acquaintances would have LOVED that turn of affairs ...

Steve: "Whatever, damned spot" is not very powerful.

Iris: Hah!

Steve: So, I think the acting coach would have us think about the people in all stages of this research project. Who would care about this topic? Once you have read what they say, why did they say that, and what are they leaving out? "What is my motivation?" is a cliché, but it can be a great question to ask about academic sources and their authors.

Iris: It is also a cliché to talk about how undergraduates are constantly asked to pretend to be little academics in their coursework, so maybe that can work in our favor, too.

Steve: Yes, I would say that I think it is fine to ask them to pretend to be junior professors. It is just a bad idea to think that they can do that without any preparation. I think it might be fun to get more "let's pretend" into our teaching.

Iris: Yes. Maybe more powerful motivation to try for inspiration as our goal might be that there is more than one kind of uninspired student. A good chunk of them might become more interested when they see that there is more going on than panning for information gold in an endless Google gold mine.

Steve: Yes, that is a good point. One of my favorite academic authors is Gerald Graff. He writes about how he was never very engaged by literature until he found out after reading *Huckleberry Finn* that it was actually a controversial work and not just a kids' story.[14] Once he had to treat a work of literature as a problem to be solved or as a cause of an argument, he suddenly found it engaging and exciting.

Of course, he then went on to be a professor of literature, so we might want to be careful—we don't want to warp all our students to that extent.

Iris: Heh. Yes, be inspiring, but not TOO inspiring.

But yes, it seems like most people go through this kind of transition, where they realize that things are deeper and more complicated than they may seem at first glance. I went through a similar moment of inspiration when I figured out that librarians do more than find stuff (like I wrote about in my essay here).

Steve: I certainly think that a liberal arts education tends to reveal the world as more complicated than it first appears, rather than providing simple answers. Which does not make it any less frustrating for us as individuals who seem to need to continually re-learn the lessons of the past. I wrote a bit in my essay about how it seems like teaching research as a part of rhetoric is something of an evergreen topic for instruction librarians. Barbara wrote the article I referenced in 1990, yet it still seems like this idea that we need to teach "information literacy" less in isolation and more in the context of critical inquiry is still a notion that we are struggling with as a profession. Do you think that is true?

Iris: I think it is true, and I was reminded of our favorite mantra that information literacy sessions are not inoculations — you cannot go to one and then know everything you need to know. So on the one hand, I am disheartened that we as a profession have not internalized this more situated, critical, and nuanced understanding of our work, but on the other hand, I think it is just as true for us as it is for our students that we need repeated interactions with the concepts throughout our careers.

The director of our writing program at Carleton has written about how ongoing faculty development on teaching writing is analogous to the ideas of "Writing Across The Curriculum," where repeated exposure and practice is more important than one perfect exposure.[15]

So that is my attempt to be optimistic about all this. The less optimistic part of me wonders if we will ever learn these lessons.

Steve: I suppose it is just parallel to what we have been talking about all along. Teaching is also something that must be learned through imaginative inquiry and constructivist knowledge creation and all that. It is easy to fall back on old habits and assumptions about what it means to teach and learn.

Iris: Yes.

Steve: Even had I read Barbara's article back in 1990, I think I would still be puzzling out all the implications and ramifications of trying to teach constructivist knowledge creation by example. That is kind of the point.

Iris: Yes, I agree, and I think I will be able to read it 5, 10, 15 years from now and it will be useful then, too.

Meanwhile, I will take your idea of being a coach and meld it with my idea of revealing the Matrix and see how that shifts my teaching. I guess that makes me Morpheus!

Steve: Hm. I am not sure putting them to sleep is a good plan.

Iris: Riiiiiight. Good point.

Steve: But I will certainly use this metaphor as an excuse to incorporate more leather and sunglasses into my teaching.

Iris: You know what they say: Pics Or It Didn't Happen.

Finis

NOTES

1. John Bean, *Engaging Ideas,* 2nd ed. (San Francisco: Jossey-Bass, 2011), 26-27.
2. Patch writing refers to the practice of gathering verbatim passages from various sources and then piecing them together, much like a patchwork quilt, with connecting words and sentences. The term was coined by Rebecca Moore Howard in *Standing in the Shadow of Giants: Plagiarists, Authors, Collaborators* (Stamford, CT: Ablex Publishers, 1999).
3. Iris Jastram, Danya Leebaw, and Heather Tompkins. "CSI(L) Carleton: Forensic Librarians and Reflective Practices," *In the Library with the Lead Pipe* (2011). http://www.inthe-librarywiththeleadpipe.org/2011/csil-carleton-forensic-librarians-and-reflective-practices/.
4. Association of College and Research Libraries, "ACRL Information Literacy Competency Standards for Higher Education" (2000), http://www.ala.org/ala/mgrps/divs/acrl/standards/informationliteracycompetency.cfm.
5. Barbara Fister, "Teaching the Rhetorical Dimensions of Research," *Research Strategies* 11, no. 4 (1993): 214.
6. Fister, "Teaching the Rhetorical Dimensions," 218.
7. Association of College and Research Libraries, "Standards."
8. Fister, "Teaching Research as a Social Act." *RQ* 29 (1990): 506.
9. Ibid.
10. Barbara Fister, "Information Literacy in a World That is Too Big to Know," *Peer-to-Peer Review—Library Journal,* 2012. http://lj.libraryjournal.com/2012/02/opinion/information-literacy-in-a-world-thats-too-big-to-know-peer-to-peer-review/.
11. See Barbara Fister, "The Research Processes of Undergraduate Students," *Journal of Academic Librarianship,* 18 no. 3 (1992).
12. "We can encourage them by example to perceive research not as a mechanical gathering process, not as a mastery of technical access tools, but as a meaningful way of making new knowledge." Fister, "Teaching Research," 509.
13. "Rather than describe the search process as a matter of finding information—which sounds like panning for solid nuggets of truth—librarians should describe it as a way of tapping into a scholarly communication network." Fister, "Teaching the Rhetorical Dimensions," 214.
14. Gerald Graff, *Beyond the Culture Wars,* (New York: W. W. Norton & Company, 1992), 67-68.
15. Carol Rutz and Jacqulyn Lauer-Glebov, "Assessment and Innovation: One Darn Thing Leads to Another," *Assessing Writing* 10, no. 2 (2005): 88.

BIBLIOGRAPHY

Association of College and Research Libraries. "ACRL Information Literacy Competency Standards for Higher Education," 2000. http://www.ala.org/ala/mgrps/divs/acrl/standards/informationliteracycompetency.cfm.

Bean, John. *Engaging Ideas*. 2nd ed. San Francisco: Jossey-Bass, 2011.

Fister, Barbara. "Teaching Research as a Social Act: Collaborative Learning and the Library." *RQ* 29, (1990): 505–509.

———. "The Research Process of Undergraduate Students." *Journal of Academic Librarianship* 18, no. 3 (1992): 163–69.

———. "Teaching the Rhetorical Dimensions of Research." *Research Strategies* 11, no. 4 (1993): 211–219.

———. "Information Literacy in a World That is Too Big to Know." *Peer-to-Peer Review—Library Journal*, 2012. http://lj.libraryjournal.com/2012/02/opinion/information-literacy-in-a-world-thats-too-big-to-know-peer-to-peer-review/.

Graff, Gerald. *Beyond the Culture Wars*. New York: W. W. Norton & Company, 1992.

Howard, Rebecca Moore. *Standing in the Shadow of Giants: Plagiarists, Authors, Collaborators*. Stamford, CT: Ablex Publishers, 1999.

Jastram, Iris, Danya Leebaw, and Heather Tompkins. "CSI(L) Carleton: Forensic Librarians and Reflective Practices." *In the Library with the Lead Pipe*, 2011. http://www.inthelibrarywiththeleadpipe.org/2011/csil-carleton-forensic-librarians-and-reflective-practices/.

Rutz, Carol, and Jacqulyn Lauer-Glebov. "Assessment and Innovation: One Darn Thing Leads to Another." *Assessing Writing* 10, no. 2 (2005): 80–99.

Nurturing Virtuous Readers

M. Patrick Graham
Margaret A. Pitts Professor of Theological Bibliography and Librarian,
Pitts Theology Library, Candler School of Theology, Emory University

For the last century, at least, American librarians have struggled to formulate a clear sense of their identity. In academic settings,[1] this usually has involved understanding their identity *vis-à-vis* faculty and administration, and obtaining "faculty status" was often seen as the optimum achievement. Depending on the institution, "faculty status" may be qualified in some way. Advances in information technology have complicated the picture even further, as librarians are increasingly required to develop strong technology skills. In many instances, professional library positions have been filled with IT professionals rather than with traditional librarians. So the target continues to move.[2]

Similarly, the mission of the library continues to shift. At one time, the majority of staff time was devoted to acquiring, cataloging, and circulating print collections. Today, the modern academic library is a campus center for technology, instruction, and socializing. Increasingly, library collections are not print or microform, but digital, and access to materials is not via an "ownership model" but through a license for a certain period and population. Librarians must now be able to negotiate such agreements, in collaboration with campus legal staff; network access, with campus IT departments; and offer instruction in their use, sometimes in collaboration with faculty. The effort to formulate, refine, and develop instructional programs under the rubric "Information Literacy Instruction" (henceforth,

ILI) has been a useful way to understand the larger academic context for libraries, and how they may contribute to the education of students.

The aim of this paper is to explore the question of how theological librarians—that particular slice of librarianship devoted to graduate theological education—may use ILI as a primary framework for pursuing the missions of their institutions. The author hopes to show how to translate the ILI program by means of the language and concepts of virtue for students in a world filled with distractions, including those aggravated by advances in information technology.[3]

Distractions

Graduate school has often been considered as a time to escape the distractions of the immediate, urgent and unimportant and devote oneself to matters of strategic and substantive importance.[4] This is especially true in our increasingly distracted world, driven by the Internet and other claims on human attention—a person's most valuable, nonrenewable resource. In schools of theology, graduate school is not just devoted to intellectual development, but accompanied by other sorts of formation. For example, the Roman Catholic Church in America has developed a highly refined program of human, intellectual, spiritual, and pastoral formation in order to train priests for ministry.[5] Protestantism and other varieties of Christianity in America pursue many of the same goals, but may not achieve the careful integration and level of development that the Catholics have, because they have not pursued it as vigorously and as long.

However, the ideal—seminary training as a time for quiet focus—is rarely the reality experienced by students. They have concerns about funding their seminary education, and often have jobs outside the classroom; expenses are a formidable issue, just as they are in American higher education in general. Family obligations loom large, because seminary students are a bit older than those in undergraduate programs, and more of them are married and have children. (There are those second-career students, often decades older than their younger peers.) In addition, theology students face heavy course loads during their three- or four-year programs (often with heavy reading assignments), and then there are the expectations of *practica* or other involvement in churches or not-for-profit programs.[6]

The point is that graduate theological students juggle many pressures and distractions from study, along with the distractions of Facebook, video-gaming, and television. In short, seminary days prepare students well for life after seminary, when they will have all these distractions and more—in particular, a congregation of persons clamoring for their attention, expressions of compassion, and leadership. If seminarians are distracted now, they will be even more distracted in the future, and will find themselves serving distracted flocks. Therefore, upon commencement, what the student will have to offer is not only what has been learned and the skills that have been mastered, but how to live productively in a world of distractions.

The literature on the Internet and distraction continues to grow, and so I will cite a couple of recent works, each making its case in a bit different way. First, Mark Bauerlein, professor of English at Emory University, has written extensively on the challenge that the Internet presents to students today. In addition to his tour de force, *The Dumbest Generation: How the Digital Age Stupefies Young Americans and Jeopardizes Our Future (or Do not Trust Anyone Under 30)*,[7] Bauerlein served as Director of the Office of Research and Analysis for the National Endowment for the Arts (2003-2005), and collaborated with others at the NEA to write, *Reading At Risk: A Survey of Literary Reading in America*,[8] which documented a decline in reading in America. Dana Gioia, chairman of the NEA, observed the following in the preface to the report, "This comprehensive survey of American literary reading presents a detailed but bleak assessment of the decline of reading's role in the nation's culture. For the first time in modern history, less than half of the adult population now reads literature, and these trends reflect a larger decline in other sorts of reading. Anyone who loves literature or values the cultural, intellectual, and political importance of active and engaged literacy in American society will respond to this report with grave concern."[9]

Bauerlein details the findings of the report, explores the habits of the young, and forecasts the implications of this new state of affairs in *The Dumbest Generation*, where he concludes, "The popular digital practices of teens and 20-year-olds did not and do not open the world. They close the doors to maturity, eroding habits of the classroom, pulling hours away from leisure practices that complement classroom habits."[10] And, who is to blame for this state of affairs? Among others, Bauerlein directs his reader's attention to "the custodians of culture, the people who serve as stewards of civilization and mentors to the next generation. They maintain the pathways into knowledge and taste—the school curriculum, cultural institutions and cultural pages in newspapers and magazines—guarding them against low standards, ahistoricism, vulgarity, and trendiness. If the pathways deteriorate, do not blame the kids and parents overmuch. Blame, also, the teachers, professors, writers, journalists, intellectuals, editors, librarians, and curators who will not insist upon the value of knowledge and tradition, who will not judge cultural novelties by the high standards set by the best of the past, who will not stand up to adolescence and announce, 'It is time to put away childish things.'"[11] So, part of the current problem with education—and librarians share part of the blame—is that worthwhile activities, such as reading books, are being crowded out by less useful things, as learning suffers and maturity is delayed.

In *The Shallows: What the Internet Is Doing to Our Brains*,[12] Nicholas G. Carr argues that, "When we go online, we enter an environment that promotes cursory reading, hurried and distracted thinking, and superficial learning."[13] Additionally, while he concurs with Bauerlein's diagnosis that Web surfing crowds out other worthwhile activities, he offers additional commentary from the world of brain science. "As the time we spend scanning Web pages crowds out the time we spend reading books, as the time we spend exchanging bite-sized text messages crowds out the time we spend composing sentences and paragraphs, as the time we spend hopping across links crowds out the time we devote to quiet reflection and contemplation, the circuits that support those old intellectual functions and pursuits weaken and begin to break apart. The brain recycles the disused neurons and synapses for other, more pressing work. We gain new skills and perspectives but lose old ones."[14] Another recent voice highlighting significant differences between books and digital texts is that of Andrew Piper, who carefully explores the physicality of the book, and the human interaction with it.[15]

While Bauerlein and Carr have their critics, of course, [16] perhaps this is enough to make the case that students in colleges, universities, and schools of theology, as well as the public generally, are increasingly distracted, and their cognitive abilities suffer accordingly. While the debate on this topic will surely continue, my immediate thesis is: Theological librarians need to do far more than simply teach their clientele how to search the web and use other electronic resources more effectively and efficiently. They need to teach them how to read deeply, engage texts and arguments critically, and do much more to equip them for life and service to their publics. The phrase that I will use for this enterprise is "nurturing virtuous readers," and reading will be understood in an expansive way to include not only deciphering symbols printed on a page or a screen, but engagement with the texts and content symbolized.[17]

The Instructional Mission of the Library

One way to think about the instructional mission of the library is to consider its role in nurturing virtuous readers. This includes providing instruction to students so that they are information literate, and so can:[18]

- Determine the extent of information needed
- Access the needed information effectively and efficiently
- Evaluate information and its sources critically
- Incorporate selected information into one's knowledge base
- Use information effectively to accomplish a specific purpose
- Understand the economic, legal, and social issues surrounding the use of information, and access and use information ethically and legally

The usefulness of ILI standards for the work of theological librarians has been treated elsewhere,[19] and so there is no need to plough that ground again here. The comprehensive program promoted by ACRL offers librarians solid counsel as they consider their instructional obligations and efforts. And the careful outline of performance indicators (instructional outcomes) enable the librarian to fully integrate ILI into their institution's larger educational program.[20] Moreover, with the strong interest in university divinity schools to teach students to think critically and theologically,[21] ILI's potential impact on teaching "critical thinking skills involving the use of information"[22] is promising. Therefore, as a document to help librarians organize and conceive their instructional work, it seems that ACRL's Information Literacy Standards are a useful tool.

However, as the theological librarian proceeds to implement it in a seminary or divinity school, it may be that some "translation" of the ACRL program would be useful. For example, terms such as "information," "knowledge base," and "access," seem somewhat antiseptic. Admittedly, such terminology is appropriate for librarians spanning many disciplines (including the humanities, social sciences, and beyond) but some adjustments may be in order to make the program more comprehensible and attractive for theology faculty and graduate students (and perhaps in the humanities generally).

As theology students are often pursuing their work with a commitment to formation (see note 5 above), they are accustomed to a different sort of language—one related to the reading and engagement of texts, wisdom, and the theological context for intellectual formation in the seminary. It may be that in university divinity schools, the ACRL language would be received more warmly, although even there, some adjustments may be in order. While these schools typically stress the importance of critical thinking and academics, there is also strong interest in engaging the students "in a theological understanding of religious traditions," preparing them "for the practice of Christian ministry," encouraging them "in their spiritual and intellectual growth," and preparing them to "be agents of social justice."[23]

Consequently, a question emerges: is there language from the world of theology or the humanities that can do justice to the concerns of information literacy, while still engaging graduate students and faculty in theological institutions of higher education? The language of technology or the social sciences may strike many as too foreign for their interests, and language that is too confessional may create additional problems for theological libraries and librarians, who also serve a wider university clientele—faculty and students from classics, philosophy, and many other fields.

The Language of Virtue

The proposal offered here comes from the humanities, and is the language of virtue. "Virtue" (Latin, *virtus*; Greek, *aretē*) may be defined as "moral excellence," and according to Aristotle (*Nicomachian Ethics*, II.1) "comes about as a result of habit" and is formed "by first exercising them [i.e., the virtues]."[24] Its history is known to students of the Greek and Roman classics, so the concept is not exclusively Christian, even though the Christian church has made extensive use of virtue language and thought in its theology and teaching. Moreover, the language of virtue has been found useful by some writing about higher education.[25] By focusing on the traditional list of four cardinal virtues—wisdom, justice, courage, and moderation— it is possible to tap into the rich moral tradition of the West, and also effectively engage Christians training for ministry.[26] The point is not to advance a parochial, Western view of morality, but to find a way to reach students undergoing formation for Christian ministry in ways that also speak to a broader or more general population using a theological library. In addition to traditional skills and knowledge typically offered by schools of theology, students will develop the habits of heart—the virtues—that enable their knowledge and skills to be practiced well, and for good.[27]

During their time in seminary, librarians hope that students will develop or sharpen their skills to search and skim the Internet quickly and efficiently, and also their abilities to read texts deeply; understand complex arguments; and be formed spiritually and intellectually in the process.[28] Preparing students to grow in this way is, of course, the responsibility of the school as a whole and requires the collaboration of faculty, librarians, and other staff. Once these students leave the university to lead congregations or not-for-profits, teach in the academy, or do other important work, they will model how to live, continue to learn, and serve in a world of distractions. They will know how to use machines, but they will not become machines, and they will not abandon their humanity. They will know how to practice their theological craft with integrity.

As an experiment in how the cardinal virtues may be used in connection with ILI, a mapping exercise may be helpful. As noted earlier, an information-literate individual is able to:[29]

1. Determine the extent of information needed
2. Access the needed information effectively and efficiently
3. Evaluate information and its sources critically
4. Incorporate selected information into one's knowledge base
5. Use information effectively to accomplish a specific purpose
6. Understand the economic, legal, and social issues surrounding the use of information, and access and use information ethically and legally

It is clear that each of these six items requires certain technical skills, but in theological schools, typically the focus is in the realm of critical thinking and assessment. For this reason, wisdom, sometimes called the "mother of the virtues,"[30] may prove helpful in mediating the list to graduate theology students. In the remarks that follow, each of the four cardinal virtues will be defined, and some suggestions about how the practice of that virtue might help advance ILI will be made.

Wisdom, or prudence, is often seen in Christian tradition as the virtue that "informs" the other virtues, which is to say that it is necessary for the practice of the others.[31] In the realm of research and libraries, for example, wisdom is required even before research gets underway. It should manifest itself in the selection of the research topic: is the topic is significant enough to merit attention? And does the student bring the requisite knowledge and skills to deal with it? This process requires a sober self-assessment and the decision not to be led by one's passion. In addition, wisdom demands that one listen to the voices of others, whether through primary sources, the secondary literature, or by soliciting the one's professor or other experts. In addition, wisdom leads one to critically engage what is read, and resist the impulse to only report on what one has read, or merely serve as a conduit for the others' judgments. Information Literacy demands that one "evaluate information and its sources critically" (item three), and this means that one reads to comprehend through reflection, perhaps incorporating it into one's understanding of what is true, then consequently changing one's views about things as necessary (item four). Wisdom also requires researchers to reserve judgment until adequate information has been gathered, and not make conclusions until hypotheses have been adequately formulated and tested. Therefore, wisdom allows the librarian to employ several of the ILI components, but to expand on them in rational and helpful ways.[32]

Justice may be defined as each person getting their due.[33] As it concerns ILI, justice requires careful citation of sources, so credit is given to those who have taught us, and we're not claiming for ourselves what belongs to someone else (item six).[34] While the admonition includes prohibitions against plagiarism, justice requires something more—a moral understanding that extends beyond law or economics. Sources must be treated fairly, not be manipulated to one's ends, and relevant material should not be suppressed or intentionally ignored. Finally, there is a personal ethic related to one's work as a researcher: one must devote adequate energy and effort to it. Laziness or slipshod research, violates the researcher's obligation to do their topic justice. In this way, justice demands scrupulous behavior towards those whose research and publications have been used, and requires the student to respect the rights of the topic or the research enterprise at hand. Once more, this virtue already informs ILI standards, but asks more of a researcher, mandating greater obligations and seriousness about the task at hand.

A third virtue, courage, may be defined as steadfastness with full knowledge of the dangers inherent in a worthwhile pursuit.[35] In the research setting, courage may allow one to develop an unpopular thesis for a research paper or publication, knowing that faculty or other readers may respond negatively to the work, since it may challenge their convictions. It may lead one to experiment or be more creative—for example, to investigate new technologies or explore new fields of inquiry—instead of playing it safe. In other contexts, it may lead one to confess ignorance, or uncertainty These may be understood to be related to items three, four, and five of the ILI standards, but some moral issues are not explicit or obvious when quickly reading through the standards.

Finally, a fourth virtue is named interchangeably moderation, temperance, or balance; it may be understood as the "inner order" of a person.[36] In the realm of ILI, this virtue finds expression when a student is not subject to impulses and passions that lead to disorder or imbalance, but is balanced within and able to assess information gathered through research, engage it fairly and objectively, and is aware of his/her own biases or presuppositions but keeping them in check so that they do not hinder the analysis. In this way, moderation prevents the academic paper from devolving into intemperate statements, or rants against other people or ideas. Such inner order makes it possible for the product of the research to be appropriate for the audience at hand, and appeal to their nobler, rational capacities. In this way, ILI standards three and five are addressed.

Summary

This experimental essay is offered to test the idea of taking the nurture of virtuous readers as the mission of a theological library. The problem afflicting the students (and those whom they serve after seminary) is distraction, or, an inability for sustained engagement with foundational and consequential texts. By employing the structure and aims of ILI, the librarian has a method for systematically guiding the students to cultivate the habit or practice of careful research, critical thinking, and intellectual integrity. Such practices, in fact, are formative and cultivate certain virtues that should serve the students well after commencement. By drawing on the rich virtue tradition of the classical authors, as mediated through early Christian writers, the librarian is able to communicate in terms relevant to seminarians the significance of the practices outlined in the ILI standards.

It is clear that the four cardinal virtues do not join neatly with ILI standards, although there are obvious points of agreement. While the latter could fit more easily with the idea of practical wisdom and mastery of processes, the cardinal virtues are more abstract, extending to elements of the research process outside of ILI standards, and sometimes interjecting additional moral elements into the research process. It is important to ask whether the use of the virtues in ILI complicates an already complex enterprise, or supports instructional aims. If the latter proves to be the case, so much the better. But if the former is true, then the theological librarian charged with implementing ILI standards would be better served by making only occasional use of the virtues to stimulate the thinking of the students, connect with their primary interests, and challenge them to serious and conscientious efforts.

NOTES

1. The focus of this paper will be on the challenges presented by academic libraries serving graduate theological education, including both university divinity schools and stand-alone seminaries.

2. See, e.g., Heidi M. Vix and Kathie M. Buckman, "Academic Librarians: Status, Privileges, and Rights," *Journal of Academic Librarianship* 38/1 (January 2012), pp. 20-25; and Martha F. Loesch, "Librarian as Professor: A Dynamic New Role Model," *Education Libraries* 33/1 (Spring 2010), pp. 31-37. Some of the more interesting conflicts among those who staff academic libraries result from the cultural differences of IT and librarianship, the prejudices of each group for the other, and the not infrequent inability of one group to understand the other. For example, the IT culture is often primarily that of a service provider and so aims at great "customer service." On the other hand, academic librarians have historically been trained to see themselves as educators and so see their relationships with students, faculty, and others in very different terms than that of providing good "customer service." They often tend to adopt something much nearer that of faculty toward students and others they serve professionally.

3. While there surely have always been distractions for those pursuing education, some see it accelerating after 1940 with the invention of television and even more so with the advent of the Internet. See, e.g., Alan Jacobs, *The Pleasures of Reading in an Age of Distraction* (Oxford: Oxford University Press, 2011), pp. 4-5.

4. Traditionally, the point has been made that "school" derives from the Latin *scholia*, which means "leisure" and that in fact scholarship requires a certain kind of leisure, viz., freedom

from the cares of earning the necessities of life in order to devote oneself to intellectual pursuits. Jacobs, *Pleasures of Reading*, p. 114.

5. United States Conference of Catholic Bishops, *Program of Priestly Formation* (Washington, D.C.; 5th edition; 2006); available online at http://www.usccb.org/beliefs-and-teachings/vocations/priesthood/priestly-formation/upload/ProgramforPriestlyFormation.pdf .

6. A survey of Candler School of Theology faculty found that "competing claims on their time—church, family, other activities…" constituted one of the two greatest "challenges or barriers to students' successful completion of assignments." Mary-Ann Winkelmes, "Location, Vocation, Formation at Candler," presentation at faculty retreat, Candler School of Theology, Aug. 17, 2012. Economic concerns have become more pronounced with undergraduates as well. Arthur Levine and Diane R. Dean, *Generation on a Tightrope: A Portrait of Today's College Student* (San Francisco: Jossey-Bass, 2012; 3rd edn.), pp. 24-27.

7. New York: Jeremy P. Tarcher/Penguin, 2008. Citations in this paper to specific pages will be to the 2011 paperback edition.

8. Research Division Report #46. (Washington, D.C.: National Endowment for the Arts, 2004). http://www.nea.gov/pub/readingatrisk.pdf

9. Ibid., p. vii.

10. Bauerlein, *Dumbest Generation*, pp; 160-61. Chapter two of the book presents the data showing that "Digital habits have mushroomed, but reading scores for teens remain flat, and measures of scientific, cultural, and civic knowledge linger at abysmal levels," p. 69.

11. Ibid., p. 161.

12. New York: W.W. Norton, 2010. See also his essay, "Is Google Making Us Stupid?" *The Atlantic* (July/August, 2008); available online at: http://www.theatlantic.com/magazine/archive/2008/07/is-google-making-us-stupid/6868/. Another interesting perspective on Carr's thesis about the impact of the Internet on reading is that of Alan Jacobs (*The Pleasures of Reading in an Age of Distraction* [New York: Oxford University Press, 2011]). See also most recently, Jennifer Howard, "The Digital World Demands a New Mode of Reading," *The Chronicle of Higher Education* (August 5, 2012); available online at: http://chronicle.com/article/The-Digital-World-Demands-a/133289/.

13. *The Shallows*, pp. 115-16; see also, p. 118.

14. Carr, *The Shallows*, p. 120. An easily accessible summary of some of the criticisms of Carr's use of neuroscience may be found in Alan Jacobs, *Pleasures of Reading*, footnote * on p. 103.

15. *Book Was There: Reading in Electronic Times* (Chicago: University of Chicago Press, 2012), pp. 14-22.

16. See, e.g., the review of *The Shallows* by Jonah Lehrer, "Our Cluttered Minds," *New York Times* (June 6, 2010), P. BR22. Online at: http://www.nytimes.com/2010/06/06/books/review/Lehrer-t.html. See also the collection of essays that illustrate some of the diverse assessments of digital tools and their use in Mark Bauerlein (ed.), *The Digital Divide* (New York: Tarcher/Penguin, 2011). "Taken together, the selections form a far-reaching body of opinion about a rushing cataclysm that has upset centuries of social and intellectual practice." *Ibid.*, p. xiii. Finally, Alan Jacobs suggests that different kinds of attention/attentiveness in reading are required for different types of literature and reading purposes, though he also notes that is may well be that one sort of reading will crowd out the others in a person's repertoire. *Pleasures of Reading*, pp. 98-102.

17. Jacobs devotes much of his book (*Pleasures of Reading*) to an explanation of what he terms "long-form reading" or "deep attention reading," viz., the sort of reading that one engages when reading a novel, and he distinguishes it from the "hyper attention" that characterizes the cramming for an exam. Pp. 106-16.

18. What follows are the Information Literacy Competency Standards for Higher Education, approved by the ACRL and cited from http://www.ala.org/acrl/standards/informationlit eracycompetency#ildef.

19. Douglas Gragg, "Information Literacy in Theological Education," *Theological Education* 40 (2004), 99-111. (http://www.pitts.emory.edu/publications/infolit.pdf). For an example of information literacy as a well-developed program, fully integrated into the research process, see William Badke, *Research Strategies: Finding Your Way through the Information Fog.* 4th Edition (http://www.acts.twu.ca/Library/textbook.htm). As for articles on ILI more generally, a survey of the literature over the two decades to 2002 found 5,009 publications, most of which dealt with ILI in higher education. Hannelore B. Rader, "Information Literacy 1973-2002: A Selected Literature Review," *Library Trends* 51/2 (2002), 242-43 (entire article, 242-59).

20. Another useful presentation of such ILI concerns is that of SCONUL (Society of College, National & University Libraries), first developed in 1999 but revised in 2011 (online at https://www.sconul.ac.uk/groups/information_literacy/publications/coremodel.pdf   ). Thanks to my colleague, Tracy P. Iwaskow, for calling this to my attention.
    - IDENTIFY: Able to identify a personal need for information
    - SCOPE: Can assess current knowledge and identify gaps
    - PLAN: Can construct strategies for locating information and data
    - GATHER: Can locate and access the information and data they need
    - EVALUATE: Can review the research process and compare and evaluate information and data
    - MANAGE: Can organize information professionally and ethically
    - PRESENT: Can apply the knowledge gained: present results of research, synthesize new and old information and data to create new knowledge and disseminate it.

21. Here and elsewhere in the paper, to think theologically is to weigh issues and topics in terms of their theological underpinning and import.

22. Abby Kasowitz-Scheer and Michael Pasqualoni, "Information Literacy Instruction in Higher Education: Trends and Issues," *Eric Digest* (2002), report number: EDO-IR-2002-01. http://www.eric.ed.gov/contentdelivery/servlet/ERICServlet?accno=ED465375 .

23. From the webpage of Vanderbilt Divinity School and Graduate Department of Religion, describing the objectives of the Divinity School. http://divinity.vanderbilt.edu/index.php (accessed 8/13/12).

24. Aristotle, *Nichomachean Ethics*; W. D. Ross, transl.; http://people.bu.edu/wwildman/ WeirdWildWeb/courses/wphil/readings/wphil_rdg09_nichomacheanethics_entire. htm.

25. Mike Higton, *A Theology of Higher Education* (Oxford: Oxford University Press, 2012), devotes a chapter of his book to "The Virtuous University," in which he distinguishes between secular and Christian virtue, elaborates intellectual virtue, and makes use of the idea of "formation in virtue." Part II, chapter 6, pp. 171-96.

26. The classical work by Josef Pieper, *The Four Cardinal Virtues* (New York: Harcourt, Brace & World, 1965), provides a helpful elaboration of the four virtues from the standpoint of Thomistic scholarship. More recently and for a broader audience, see Mary M. Keyes, *Aquinas, Aristotle, and the Promise of the Common Good* (Cambridge; New York: Cambridge University Press, 2006), who examines the relation of personal and common goods and makes the case for the social and civic value of the four cardinal virtues. As an example of these virtues for the world of commerce, see Robert W. Lane, "Vigorous Competition, Cardinal Virtues, and Value Creation," ch. 6 in Robert P. Gandossy and Jeffrey A. Sonnenfeld

(eds.), *Leadership and Governance from the Inside Out* (Hoboken, N.J.: J. Wiley, 2004). Finally, on the usefulness of the cardinal virtues for contemporary ethics generally, see Richard J. White, *Radical Virtues: Moral Wisdom and the Ethics of Contemporary Life* (Lanham, Md.: Rowman & Littlefield, 2008).

27. Beth Mole's recent article in the *Chronicle for Higher Education* "How to Train Graduate Students in Research Ethics: Lessons from 6 Universities," (available online at http://chronicle.com/article/How-to-Train-Graduate-Students/133623/?cid=at&utm_source=at&utm_medium=en) calls attention to the work of the Council of Graduate Schools and its Project for Scholarly Integrity, from which the report *Research and Scholarly Integrity in Graduate Education: A Comprehensive Approach* has just been issued (CGS, 2012; http://www.cgsnet.org/project-scholarly-integrity).

28. Higton (*Theology of Higher Education*) articulates a vision of university education as an apprenticeship for the student: "…formation in virtue is bound to take the form of *apprenticeship*. …in a system of virtue, excellence is primarily embodied in persons and only secondarily in the products of their virtue (excellent works and judgements[sic?]) or in codification of what it is about their works that make them excellent…." (181) "…all university learning properly takes the form of learning a craft … [it] has to involve the formation of extended relationships between masters and apprentices…." (182) Similarly, it is hardly a long step to conceive of librarians engaging students in a similar kind of apprenticeship, as they teach them proper research techniques.

29. See note 14 above.

30. Pieper, *The Four Cardinal Virtues*, p. 3.

31. Pieper, *The Four Cardinal Virtues*, pp. 5-7.

32. More generally with regard to the ILI standards, it is clear that practical wisdom—the knowing how to do something well and for good, such as determining the nature and extent of the information needed—could cover all the standards, just as the virtue of wisdom is required in the practice of the other virtues.

33. Pieper, *The Four Cardinal Virtues*, p. 44.

34. Among the more egregious examples of plagiarism is illustrated by the recent account of Dave Tomer's extensive business of writing papers for hire. *The Shadow Scholar: How I Made a Living Helping College Kids Cheat* (New York: Bloomsbury, 2012). The recent article by Jeff Karon ("A Positive Solution for Plagiarism," *The Chronicle of Higher Education* [September 21, 2012] http://chronicle.com/article/A-Positive-Solution-for/134498/) on the topic of plagiarism takes a refreshingly positive approach and uses the language of virtue: "…my goal should be to help inculcate honor and integrity rather than build a culture of fear and accusation."

35. In some life circumstances it may be the "readiness to fall in battle." Pieper, *The Four Cardinal Virtues*, pp. 117-21. Harvey C. Mansfield's book, *Manliness* (New Haven: Yale University Press, 2006) defines "manliness" (Greek, *andreia*; the term used by Aristotle for "courage" in *Nicomachean Ethics*, II.2) as "confidence in the face of risk" (p. 23).

36. Pieper, *The Four Cardinal Virtues*, pp. 145-46, 203. "The primary and essential meaning of *temperare*, therefore, is this: to dispose various parts into one unified and ordered whole" (p. 146).

Student-centered Library Use

Joanne Hélouvry
Head of Research & Instruction Services, Loyola—Notre Dame Library,
Loyola University Maryland, Notre Dame of Maryland University

Walking through the first floor of the library today, I saw the space being used in a variety of ways. One student, sitting at a table near the reference desk, was reading a volume of Proust. A live-in pharmacy graduate student had her laptop flipped up, and was frantically researching at a table near the reference desk. Another student was spread out at one of the computers, library books and course books piled up, his banana and Famous Amos cookies strategically placed just above the keyboard. And a fourth was perched on the soft seats near the magazines, legs hiked over the edge, thumbing through the current issue of Cosmo. The Loyola Notre Dame Library was remodeled and expanded in 2008, and one can clearly see that students feel at home in the space we have created for them. Barbara Fister states that "[t]he library provides an anchor for [students]: a place they can return to several times a day to rest, study, meet friends, check their e-mail, download assignments, gather sources, and write papers. Quite often, they can't find time in their schedules to settle down to sustained research and writing until classes and scheduled activities are over—usually after 9 p.m."[1]

Libraries, traditionally the repositories of print collections, now provide electronic access to a wide range of digital resources. Yet, instead of threatening the traditional concept of the library, the integration of information technology has actually become a catalyst for transforming the library into a more vital and critical intellectual center of life at colleges and universities today.[2] While students have always used the library to study, how does the academic library continue to provide for student learning within the library building, and what methods are being used to explore evolving needs? What changes are libraries making to physical spaces and the social atmosphere of the library that allow easier and more inviting access to resources? With assessment on the rise in academia, how are librarians [highlighting/revealing/showing?] the actual value of the academic library to students, university administrators, and other stakeholders? This chapter examines the changing academic library as a physical space for student learning and social interaction.

In the last ten years, the term "Library as Place" has become ubiquitous in the library literature. Since the Council on Library and Information Resources published their report in 2005,[3] the concept has broadened to encompass many elements. As academic communities evolve and technology evolves in relation to them, libraries have become elements of the *social* fabric of schools, not just places that house intellectual capital. Looking at how students study, the ways they use the library, and their changing learning behaviors, allows us to better determine how libraries can meet student needs. One model that is standard in the academic library is the "information commons," or "learning commons."

Learning Commons

The phrase "information commons" was coined at the beginning of the new millennium. Conceived as a place that students could gather; access and utilize technologies; and receive help from librarians, information commons were modeled off of large academic computer labs that became commonplace in the 1990s. Don Beagle, an early proponent, states that this new space "...offers a 'continuum of service' that can help the student move through and then beyond the established regime of information access and retrieval, through further steps of interpretation, processing and manipulation...."[4] This formulation clearly shows a shift in the last 10 years from simply providing technological resources—as in the initial information commons—toward a broader and more holistic "learning commons." Beagle observes that we "all understand that a media booth does not turn a student into a scholar—nor does a seminar room or even a writing tutor. But when these and other elements are combined within a reconceptu- alized service framework and projected onto a reconfigured library floor plan, the result can mesh with creative pedagogy to become something that seems greater than these constituent parts."[5]

The literature repeatedly features models of information commons that emphasize the centrality of student learning in their designs, as evidenced by an entire issue of the *Journal of Library Administration* published in January 2010.[6] Today, faculty direct students toward team-based learning structures in their coursework; as a space, the learning commons plays an active role in supporting this type of student learning. The idea of "inten- tional learning"—when students are actively engaged in conscious acqui- sition and use of knowledge outside of the classroom—is a new and im- portant area of study.[7] Bennett's work on in-depth learning finds that in most surveyed schools, student and faculty respondents "most frequently regarded libraries as fostering learning behaviors important to them." In short, the library is seen as the place where learning outside the classroom most frequently occurs.[8] Librarians as facilitators to classroom learning is another emerging trend in academia. While this article does not delve into the rise of the information literacy movement, the parallel rise of the learn- ing commons—which can include librarians working more closely with faculty to cement connections between courses and library resources— suggests the increasing prevalence of informal, out-of-class, library-based learning.

Lippincott notes that the learning commons gained favor as "millennial" students entered universities. She observes that this association is "likely a close synergy between the characteristics of the Information Commons and the way that millennial students conduct their academic and social lives. Information Commons provide reinforcement for the social aspects of learning, offer abundant technology and digital content, and provide students with a physical setting that is often available."[9] The quiet library of the previous five hundred years is no more. Instead, the library has become a vibrant, social space that is able to accommodate diverse student learning needs.

Librarians have many resources for learning how to create learning commons and other spaces conducive to student learning. The "Learning Space Tool Kit" is one example of an intensive program formulated to help create "places that accommodate a wide range of activities, technologies, and participants—both in-person and connected virtually." The tool kit authors observe that people "need to be able to create, retrieve, combine, display, share information, then do it all over again, all in a space that they can easily reconfigure and is well supported by staff that meet and anticipate their needs."[10] Tools such as needs assessments, space type identification, and guiding principles help get librarians up to speed.

Library architects have also taken these changing needs into account. Studies such as Libqual+[11] and the MISO[12] survey—which ask if and how library spaces inspire study and learning, and how often library spaces and resources are used—address the technological, spatial, and individual study needs of students. Much has been said in the literature about the value of gathering data about student use through quantitative surveys. Incorporating students in this kind of research project can spur excitement about the library, while leading to a better understanding of student needs. Librarians at the Auraria Library, which serves the University of Colorado Denver, Metropolitan State College of Denver, and the Community College of Denver, collaborated with several academic classes on participatory action research. "As a result of the action research ... the Auraria Library put together a plan for [a] renovation that included a list of student-identified improvements. Funding is limited and the renovation has to be scheduled in phases as money becomes available with an emphasis on improvements that are the most cost effective. Ideas that have been implemented [immediately included] [r]eplac[ing] tall bookshelves with shorter bookshelves. Mov[ing] seating areas to the edges of the buildings to take advantage of the many windows in the building, [p]urchas[ing] furniture in a variety of styles to cater to different preferences and types of activities." These findings suggested that simple and easily implemented changes enhance the learning environment, make it more comfortable, and promote library use.[13]

Ethnography

Ethnographic research into library use by students has grown exponentially in the last 10 years. Khoo, Rozaklis, and Hall (2012) surveyed 81 studies of ethnographic research done in libraries since 1980, and found an upward spike to be in 2005-2006. Their study indicates that there is a "growing interest in qualitative analyses of the social lives of libraries, and the roles that libraries play in the lives of their users...."[14] Ethnography allows for interesting explorations of student library use, including cartographic mapping, photographic studies, observation, cultural probes (with student input), and focus groups.[15] In 2006, Lynda Baker spoke about observation as the "systematic recording of observable phenomena or behavior in a natural setting." Instead of passive observation, Baker takes a very active role as a researcher, working closely with study participants; developing personal connection with the participants; and using all senses in observations.[16]

Nancy Foster and Susan Gibbons delve into student studying practices and connections to the library in "Studying Students." Judi Briden's photo project, included in the Foster and Gibbons report, led her to "discover the unexpected, creat[ing] artifacts that [could] be used as a basis for discussion," and enabled her to "learn about different parts of students' lives we would not learn about through conversation."[17] In response to questions about the library and study habits, Briden learned about students to take photos of favorite spaces, or confusing areas. Then, she interviewed the students about their photographs. Because she could see their images— the students took the pictures in dorms and other study spaces, and discovered alternate study spaces outside of the library—Briden found that she could better understand student perceptions. "As we asked questions about what we could see in the images," writes Briden, "we learned how students did their work and what they did for recreation and relaxation. We learned about social interactions with roommates and floor mates and friends. The many objects shown, and their juxtaposition, prompted us to ask questions we had not anticipated, but that turned out to be very informative."[18] "The library provided a refuge when students just *had* to work."[19]

Hobbs and Klare wanted to determine the best study spaces for students, and informed by Foster and Gibbons' photographic research, they looked at what made a space comfortable and conducive for studying, or the opposite.[20] Using photographic and other methods, they made choices about setting up library study spaces. Whether graduate and undergraduate students, or students with different majors, the study demonstrated that student populations have different needs thus each of their libraries invited different space design.[21]

The ERIAL study (Ethnographic Research in Illinois Academic Libraries), completed by five Illinois universities from 2008 to 2010, examined how students view and use their campus libraries.[22] The Ames Library at Illinois Wesleyan University made many changes in response to the study. After realizing the word 'reference'—as in 'reference desk'—had no meaning for students, the reference desk and reference collection were physically removed.

"The materials in the reference collection are now in the stacks, and some of those items circulate," said University Librarian and Professor Karen Schmidt. "Students now find reference material alongside the regular collections. This encourages serendipitous discovery.'"[23]

Treadwell, Binder, and Tagge, from University of Illinois Springfield used the ERIAL study examine how students viewed the library. They found that students appreciated areas such as:"the coffee shop, the lounges, some of the study spaces in the stacks, and the ubiquity of computers throughout the building. Looking to the future, students wanted to see a more open and inviting space, more group study rooms, spaces clearly marked for group study, noise, and socializing, and clearer organization and way-finding.... One of the most intriguing ideas, which affirmed a direction that the design committee was taking, was that 'everything geared to studying should be in the library."[24]

An ideal library would seem to combine learning and social spaces, and create opportunities for students to come together, or escape to solitary places (figure 6.1).

Figure 6.1. Loyola Notre Dame Library Second Floor Open Plan Seating

Social Spaces

Francine May examines the different methods to examine social spaces in the library by using a "patron-centered perspective." She speaks to the large body of research on libraries as informal gathering spaces, and comments on each library's unique qualities and situations. May observes that the "[i]nformation gathered from use-of-space research can be used for a variety of purposes, from feeding into design and renovation projects to contributing to library promotion and funding initiatives."[25]

The Goucher College Athenaeum in Towson, Maryland, is an example of a library space that has been designed with user-friendliness in mind; The space—which houses the library, an art gallery, the campus radio station, a café, work-out area, and large open amphitheater— is designed for multiple uses, and accommodates individual study carrels, group study spaces, and even bean bag chairs for relaxing and study[26] (figure 6.2).

Figure 6.2. Goucher College Athaneum: Bean Bag Seating[27]

The Johns Hopkins University Brody Learning Commons and Loyola University Chicago's Richard J. Klarchek Information Commons are bright, open spaces, connected to the library. These spaces are uniquely designed for individual and group study, and are meant to be comfortable, functional as well as serving as places to "learn, share, connect, create and relax."[28] Nevertheless, the library as a place to relax and socialize is a concept that has only taken root over the past decade. Pleasure

reading is one way of attracting students. Gilbert and Fister state: [a]ca-
demic libraries provide academic resources for students while they are
enrolled, but they also hope to promote habits of lifelong learning.... If
we want our students to continue to read after college, we should look
beyond helping them succeed as students, but also consider ways to help
them develop their personal reading tastes, learn effective ways to identify satisfying reading material, and instill an expectation that they can
turn to libraries after college for their continued education and development.[29] More and more, the academic library is expected to provide many
services provided by public libraries, such as book clubs, author events,
and other promotions and support. Often, these services are linked to
diversity reading book clubs on campus, the common campus read, and
current events. Promoting extracurricular reading to college students has
been shown to improve literacy rates, which, in turn, may relate to higher
rates of employment among college graduates.[30] The coffee bar—now
quite common in academic libraries—is an example of a new service.
After Barnes & Noble teamed with Starbucks in the 1990s for a wildly
successful partnership, many academic libraries began to relax rules
and strictures. Libraries began to reinvent themselves, and change from
stodgy places of study to friendly, open, and social spaces. Public and academic libraries created spaces for relaxation, and soft seating and groups
of couches have been incorporated to provide areas where patrons can
pop open a laptop, a magazine, or a book in comfort. For example, Libraries such as the "University of North Carolina at Greensboro (UNCG)
University Libraries [have] developed the 'Student Affairs Connection'
program in order to market the Libraries to students in co-curricular settings and to collaborate more closely with the Student Affairs Division."[31]
UNCG libraries sponsor game nights, have initiated a Student Libraries
Advisory Council, and are present at activities and fairs. And, better gaug-
ing of student needs has increased gate counts at UNCG by 164% in just
two years.[32]

Reducing stress has also been a goal for librarians at Erie College of Penn-
sylvania. They instituted a program to serve free coffee during finals to at-

tract students. This was a successful experiment; students were grateful and happy, and the program attracted students who had never used the library, but who decided to visit "just for the free coffee."[33] The University of North Carolina at Charlotte, University of Connecticut, and California State University-San Marcos have used therapy dogs in and outside of the library so students can pet the dogs and take breaks during final exams.[34] This practice has continued for multiple semesters and generated positive feedback from students, faculty, and administration about the effectiveness of relaxing with a furry friend.

Graduate Student Needs

While all students need to relax and study, graduate students tend to have different needs than undergraduate students. According to Beard and Bawden, graduate students "require silent study space, are enthusiastic book borrowers, and have limited interest in social media in the library."[35] Kayongo and Helm, however, state that graduate students are most interested in library resources—primarily from online sources—and study space ranks low on their list of priorities.[36] Beard and Bawden state that the library has become "less valid as a physical space due to the fact that many have their own space, be that an office or at home, and, due to the self study element of being a [graduate] research student the need for the structure that a library brings is not as high. Something that is a worrying trend for the academic libraries is the fact that what appears to be a large number of research students regard themselves as not using any library resources at all."[37]

They do suggest that graduate students are an undermarketed group, and that libraries should work to promote specific resources, areas, and services to them. Some libraries with large graduate programs—such as Kansas State University and University of California, Berkeley—do target graduate populations. Berkeley offers a core non-circulating research collection to support UC Berkeley's graduate programs in the humanities and history. K-State librarians assist with theses and dissertation research, and librarians at Loyola Notre Dame consult with each doctoral education student at Notre Dame of Maryland University to refine their literature review. These services promote the use of the library spaces and resources by graduate students.[38]

Library Value

In the last 10 years, higher education commissions and universities have placed greater emphasis on student learning assessments in undergraduate education, and this has yielded enormous quantities of statistics. Offices of institutional research have accumulated large quantities of data that can be used to inform librarians' understanding of student use of libraries. Megan Oakleaf, in "The Value of Academic Libraries," speaks to the best practices currently being used in researching the performance of academic libraries. The report suggests "[t]o investigate the ways in which libraries currently ... contribute to student achievement, librarians can partner with campus colleagues in order to leverage existing data sources, including registrar records, institutional test score reports, test item audits, and records of individual students' library behaviors." She offers 22 "Next Steps" recommendations for academic librarians who wish to demonstrate value. These recommendations, along with a comprehensive research agenda, lay out areas of library value and link them to types of assessment that can be done in academic settings. She states

> For example, student enrollment is one area of institutional value. Surrogates for library impact on student enrollment include the recruitment of prospective students, matriculation of admitted students, and willingness of current students to recommend the institution to others. In other words, libraries can demonstrate their value by providing evidence that they play a role in student recruitment, matriculation, and willingness to recommend. They can do that by participating in prospective student events or new student orientation, assigning librarians as student advisors, or offering services that positively impact student judgments of institutional quality.[39]

Even as donors and other stakeholders ask universities are being asked to show how libraries are being used, the value of the library continues to grow. For example, the University of Minnesota conducted an in-depth analysis of library value using data—correlating library use with students' grade point average—accumulated by their office of institutional research. By crunching numbers on workstation use, book checkouts, and library website use and GPA from different university departments, their findings showed that the more students used the library, the higher student GPA tended to be. This kind of evidence is incredibly valuable, and helpful in making the case for funding to improve library spaces, and to market the library to students.[40]

Nancy Marlin, Provost at San Diego State University, describes one way libraries can use these statistics to promote library use to a specific student group in this case, commuter students.

> "[F]rom the data we have, where are the particular needs? ... What if we really create a space for these commuter students that would connect them peer to peer? We do some academic work. We put them in learning communities, sort of the same classes. They have this space in the library that would be for them. We have the resources that the librarians can bring to bear to help those students ... to create an engagement, even though they aren't living on campus. Maybe we will have lockers where they can plug in their laptops and things like that."[41]

This is an example of innovative and out-of-the-box thinking about student needs, and how the library might best address them.

Librarians are urged to remember that the library goals are based on facilitating student learning. As the research shows, drawing students into the conversation on services and spaces that best support their optimal learning is the key to engaging students within academic library environments. As Freeman asserts in the "Library as Place" report, when planning for a new or renovated library building, the team must ground their process in the institution's mission, goals, and values, and not simply follow a current and popular template.[42] Johns Hopkins University has created a position focused uniquely on this concept entitled the "Student Engagement and Information Skills Librarian." "This position plans, designs, implements, reviews, and assesses programs and services that foster the research needs of students, with an emphasis on undergraduates….This position will… build partnerships and programs that support student learning through positive engagement with students in both formal and informal settings."[43]

Clearly, academic libraries of the future must be invested in student development and growth. As Barbara Fister states, "Our libraries are places that learners lay claim to as a base camp, cartographers beginning an adventure into the unknown. We only need to welcome them inside so they can find a table and a window and make it their own."[44]

NOTES

1. Fister, Barbara, "The Glorious Study Hall: How Libraries Nurture a Life of the Mind," *Library Issues: Briefings for Faculty and Administrators* 30, no. 2 (2009).
2. Geoffrey T. Freeman, "The Library as Place: Changes in Learning Patterns, Collections, Technology, and Use," in *Library as Place: Rethinking Roles, Rethinking Space* (Washington, DC: Council on Library and Information Resources, 2005), 1-9.
3. The CLIR report is intended to stimulate thinking about the role of the library in the digital age, about the potential—and the imperative—for libraries to meet new needs, and about how these needs will influence the design of physical space. Council on Library and Information Resources, "Preface," *Library as Place: Rethinking Roles, Rethinking Space,* Washington, DC: Council on Library and Information Resources, 2005. For more information on Library as Place see also The American Library Association wiki page bibliography defining and citing articles on Library as Place. American Library Association, "Library as Place," *American Library Association,* accessed January 12, 2013, http://wikis.ala.org/professionaltips/index.php?title= Library_as_Place.
4. Donald Beagle, "The Emergent Information Commons: Philosophy, Models, and 21st Century Learning Paradigms," *Journal of Library Administration* 50, no. 1 (January 2010), 9-10.
5. Ibid, 8.
6. In the introduction to the January 2010 issue of *Journal of Library Administration,* Robert A. Seal, Dean of Libraries at Loyola University Chicago, explains that the issue brings together "articles on the topic by practitioners with experience in creating, managing and improving the service model that one writer aptly called a 'centralized location where the common activity is to find, use and create information.'"
7. Scott Bennett looks at learning and learning behaviors in six institutions to address spaces students use to conduct actual learning. He examines ten types of intentional learning behaviors, drawing from the National Survey of Student Engagement, that allow students to complete higher level learning functions, and examines the spaces students use. These learning paradigms included the three most important approaches: group study, individual study, and side-by-side study. Bennett says that library space design must incorporate an

understanding that individual and collaborative study are essential to learning. Scott Bennett, "Learning Behaviors and Learning Spaces." *Portal: Libraries & the Academy* 11, no. 3 (2011): 783.

8. Ibid, 776.
9. Joan K. Lippincott, "Information Commons: Meeting Millennials' Needs," *Journal of Library Administration* 50, no. 1 (January 2010): 27-37.
10. Learning Space Tool Kit, accessed January 14, 2013, http://learningspacetoolkit.org/
11. Multiple articles have been published on using Libqual+ and Library as Place results to inform space planning decisions. The Libqual+ survey asks multiple Library as Place questions, including: Is the library a center for intellectual stimulation? Is it a place for reflection & creativity? Does the library space inspire study and teaching? Is the library a comfortable and inviting location? A few of the articles reviewed are: Jan Lewis, "Using LibQual+ to Inform Space Planning Decisions," LibQual+ Share Fair Conference (July 13, 2009) http://www.libqual.org/documents/LibQual/publications/ShareFair_2009_EastCarolina.pdf.; Jacqui Dowd, "LibQual+ and the 'Library as Place' at the University of Glasgow," *Research Library Issues: A Bimonthly Report from ARL, CNI, and SPARC*, no. 271 (August 2010); 13-20; Pedramnia, S., P. Modiramani, and V.G. Ghanbarabadi, "An analysis of service quality in academic libraries using LibQUAL scale: Application oriented approach, a case study in Mashhad University of Medical Sciences (MUMS) libraries," *Library Management* 33, no. 3 (January 1, 2012): 159-167.
12. MISO (Measuring Information Service Outcomes) Survey. Accessed January 12, 2013, http://www.misosurvey.org/
13. Margaret Brown-Sica, "Using Academic Courses to Generate Data for use in Evidence Based Library Planning." *The Journal of Academic Librarianship.* (In press, accepted manuscript, January 11, 2013): 10. doi:10.1016/j.acalib.2013.01.001
14. Michael Khoo, Lily Rozaklis, and Catherine Hall, "A Survey of the Use of Ethnographic Methods in the Study of Libraries and Library Users," *Library and Information Science Research* 34, (2012): 82-91.
15. Ibid, 86.
16. Lynda M. Baker, "Observation: A Complex Research Method," *Library Trends* 55, no. 1 (Summer 2006): 171.
17. Judi Briden, "Photo Surveys: Eliciting More than You Knew to Ask for," In *Studying Students: The Undergraduate Research Project at the University of Rochester*, edited by Nancy Fried Foster, and Susan Gibbons, (Chicago: Association of College and Research Libraries), 41.
18. Ibid, 45.
19. Ibid, 47.
20. Kendall Hobbs and Diane Klare, "User-Driven Design: Using Ethnographic Techniques to Plan Student Study Space," *Technical Services Quarterly* 27, no. 4 (October 2010): 350.
21. Ibid.
22. Ethnographic Research in Illinois Academic Libraries. Accessed January 12, 2013 from http://www.erialproject.org/.
23. Kim Hill, "Students' Study Habits Prompt Changes at The Ames Library" Illinois Wesleyan University Office of Communications, News and Events. Accessed January 13, 2103. http://www.iwu.edu/news/2013/01-library-research-skills.html.
24. Jane Treadwell, Amanda Binder, and Natalie Tagge, "Seeing Ourselves as Others See Us: Library Spaces through Student Eyes," In *College Libraries and Student Culture: What we Now Know*, edited by Lynda M. Duke and Andrew D. Asher, Chicago: American Library

Association, 2011, 132.

25. Francine May, "Methods for Studying the Use of Public Spaces in Libraries." *Canadian Journal Of Information & Library Sciences* 35, no. 4 (December 2011), 355.

26. Scott Carlson, "Is it a Library? A Student Center? The Athenaeum Opens at Goucher College," *Chronicle of Higher Education,* September 18, 2009, A16.

27. Photo courtesy of Goucher College.

28. Johns Hopkins University Brody Learning Commons: http://releases.jhu.edu/2012/09/04/ brody-learning-commons-opens-at-johns-hopkins-homewood-campus/. Also, Loyola University Chicago's Richard J. Klarcheck Information Commons: http://luc.edu/ic.

29. Julie Gilbert and Barbara Fister, "Reading Risk, and Reality: College Students and Reading for Pleasure." *College and Research Libraries* 72, no. 5 (2011), 490.

30. Barry Trott and Julie Elliott, "Barriers to Extracurricular Reading Promotion in Academic Libraries," *Reference & User Services Quarterly* 48, no. 4 (Summer, 2009), 340-346; Barry Trott and Martin Goldberg, "Extracurricular Reading," *Reference & User Services Quarterly* 51, no. 3 (Spring, 2012), 231-234.

31. Kathryn M. Crowe, "Student Affairs Connection: Promoting the Library through Co-Curricular Activities," *Collaborative Librarianship* 2, no. 3 (07, 2010), 154.

32. Ibid, 157.

33. Russell A. Hall, Jane Ingold, and Richard Hart, "Fuel for Finals." *College & Research Libraries News* 73, no. 9 (10, 2012),: 544-546.

34. Jean Hiebert and Shelly Theriault, "BLASTing the Zombies!: Creative Ideas to Fight Finals Fatigue," *College & Research Libraries News* 73, no. 9 (2012)540-543.; Jo Ann Reynolds and Laurel Rabschutz, "Studying for Exams just Got More Relaxing: Animal-Assisted Activities at the University of Connecticut Library," *College & Undergraduate Libraries* 18, no. 4 (Oct, 2011): 359-367.; Conversation with Barbara Preece, Director of CSU, San Marcos, January 10, 2-13.

35. Colin Beard and David Bawden, "University Libraries and the Postgraduate Student: Physical and Virtual Spaces," *New Library World* 113, no. 9 (2012): 439.

36. Jessica Kayongo and Clarence Helm, "Graduate Students and the Library: A Survey of Research Practices and Library Use at the University of Notre Dame," *Reference & User Services Quarterly* no. 4 (2010): 344.

37. Colin Beard and David Bawden, "University Libraries and the Postgraduate Student: Physical and Virtual Spaces," *New Library World* 113, no. 9 (2012), 444.

38. University of California Berkeley Library, Doe & Moffitt Libraries Graduate Services, accessed March 19, 2013, http://www.lib.berkeley.edu/doemoff/grad/.; K-State Libraries Faculty and Graduate Services, accessed March 19, 2013, http://www.lib.k-state.edu/depts/facgrad/index.html.

39. Megan Oakleaf, *Value of Academic Libraries: A Comprehensive Research Review and Report,* Chicago: Association of College and Research Libraries, 2010, 114. For more information, see also the Association of College & Research Libraries Value of Academic Libraries Blog. Accessed January 12, 2013, http://www.acrl.ala.org/value/.

40. Jan Franzen, Kristen Mastel, Shane Nackerud, Kate Peterson, David Peterson, and Krista Soria, Library Data and Student Success. Presentation at the Maryland Value of Academic Libraries Meeting, Columbia, MD, October 5, 2102. http://digitalcommons.macalester.edu/cgi/ viewcontent.cgi?article=1221&context=libtech_conf.

41. Value of Academic Libraries Podcast, Nancy Marlin, March 8, 2012. http://www.acrl.ala.org/ value/?p=265.

42. Geoffrey T. Freeman, "The Library as Place: Changes in Learning Patterns, Collections, Technology, and Use," in *Library as Place: Rethinking Roles, Rethinking Space* (Washington, DC: Council on Library and Information Resources, 2005), 6.

43. Kathleen Kessler to Marylib mailing list, January 15, 2013. https://lists.umaryland.edu/sympa/arc/marylib/2013-01/msg00015.html.

44. Barbara Fister, "Libraries and the Cartography of Knowledge," presentation to the Alaska Library Association Conference, Anchorage, AK, February 23-26, 2006. http://homepages.gac.edu/~fister/cartography.html.

Building Bridges from the Ivory Tower

Anne-Marie Deitering

Franklin McEdward Professor for Undergraduate Learning Initiatives, OSU Libraries and Press, Oregon State University

Introduction

The *Oxford English Dictionary* defines the phrase "ivory tower" as "[a] condition of seclusion or separation from the world; in general, protection or shelter from the harsh realities of life."[1] The definition sounds like a nice place—a place anyone would want to be—but for its entire history, this term has been used pejoratively. The assumption that the work of the university takes place in this ivory tower, separate from the "real world," is longstanding and pervasive. And the image of the solitary scholar, engaged in Deep Thoughts and unconcerned with the daily cares of real people, is a familiar one. Examples abound of pundits choosing ridiculous-sounding dissertation titles to show that scholarly inquiry is unworthy of popular support. Online discussions are derailed when academic research is dismissed because, being academic, it could not possibly relate to the real world.

We live in a world where the work of scholars could inform public discourse, but it frequently does not. One response to this disconnect is to criticize the scholars—to accuse them of hiding behind the ivory tower walls, and assume they are refusing to engage with the broader public. While there certainly may be some truth to that observation, the real story is far more complex.

Librarians stand with one foot in both worlds; they are engaged in the regular work of day-to-day practice, and play an essential role in the scholarly enterprise. Librarians work with researchers as they create new knowledge, buy back the fruits of that labor in the form of books and journals, and help students make their first connections to the world of scholarship. In this essay, I will argue that how we do that last piece is essential.

Too often, undergraduate students learn to use scholarly resources in ways that reinforce their alleged irrelevance to the "real world." When our students are required to use scholarly sources in ways that are divorced from the disciplinary discourse communities that produce them; when they are told they must use peer-reviewed articles, but given no explanations why; when their research becomes a matter of checking off source types and formatting citations; they do not learn why the research skills we teach (and the sources we collect) are valuable even outside the classroom.

As librarians, we have unique perspectives on scholarship and the value of scholarly information. Like most of our students, we are generalists. Like most of our students, we need to figure out how to use, evaluate, and sift through scholarly sources without being experts ourselves. We need to use these perspectives to ensure that our students explore scholarly sources in an authentic way. As Barbara Fister argued in 2010:

> We cannot just provide content; we need to help novice researchers find the good stuff without resorting to rote routine or expecting them to simply search more databases more thoroughly. We need to question what life-long purpose learning to use academic content in academic libraries actually has. We need to ask what value academic inquiry has, period.[2]

Barbara Fister has been asking these questions, and answering them, for years. And her model shows that we need to explore these answers beyond the library and beyond the classroom, and we need to explore them together with faculty and students. As Barbara said to her *Inside Higher Ed* audience in 2012,

> If I didn't think scholarship matters in the real world, if I didn't
> think it has lasting value, then my job as a librarian, working
> with students who mostly will not become academics, would
> lack all meaning.[3]

Finding that lasting value, and making sure that what we do within the
ivory tower connects to the real worlds beyond, is a crucial role for librarians in the 21st century.

The Ivory Tower & the Real World

In the summer of 2012, the public's imagination was captured by two de-
cidedly scientific stories: the successful landing of NASA's Mars Rover,
Curiosity, and the discovery of the Higgs-Boson-like "god particle." Events
like these show that people outside of the academy are still capable of getting swept away in the excitement of scientific discovery. Still, the excitement surrounding these exceptional events has not led to a widespread
belief that scientific research or scholarly knowledge has relevance to our
daily lives.

Indeed, it is difficult to avoid the conclusion that there is significant and
growing disdain in our culture for scientific research and evidence. In
2011, critical pedagogy theorist Henry Giroux put it this way: the general
public "appears increasingly united in its dismissal of 'Ivory Tower' elites
who are viewed as speaking and writing in a discourse that is as arcane as
it is irrelevant."[4] It cannot be denied that this discourse is difficult for the
general public to access. As Christie Wilcox argues in an editorial in the
Biological Bulletin, scientific knowledge is usually locked away in journals
that are too expensive for the average person to buy. And even when the
public can get past publishers' paywalls, they can still be derailed by "jargon walls"—the specialized, linguistic shortcuts that scholars use because
they assume they are writing for each other, not for a wider audience.[5]

This perspective, that scholarly discourse is too technical, jargon-rich and
arcane for wide understanding, is common. In an editorial at Nature.com,
Kate Pratt summarizes it neatly:

How is it that in the face of cold, hard, data the public often chooses to ignore or flat out refute scientific evidence? After all, shouldn't the facts speak for themselves? It seems that these questions do not bother scientists enough. They often shrug off the latest miscommunication in the press as the fault of some lazy journalist who didn't read the press release correctly. They do not consider that they are perhaps to blame, and, instead of trying to improve their communication skills with the lay-public, they withdraw quietly into the protective shell that is academia.[6]

It is easy to say that scholars should write more simply and engage more directly with the public, but easy solutions are rarely effective when problems are this complex. There are many reasons why scholars do not do these things. Richard Demillo (2011) locates one of these in the huge influx of federal money that flowed into universities and research centers after World War II. As higher education became increasingly reliant on these federal dollars a new kind of professor rose to prominence, particularly in the STEM fields: one who could attract and manage research dollars. Every step of the federal grant-allocation process—from the initial requests for funding to the publication of results in scholarly journals—is governed by peer review. It is the ability to effectively communicate with peers, not with the public, that is essential for success in this environment.[7] A recent conversation on the blog Soapboxscience highlights the restrictions this funding model places on scholars who want to engage with the public. As one commenter puts it:

> I want to come out in defense of scientists. I am growing weary of the blame being placed on them (me) for not 'breaking it down' for public audiences. All too often, scientists are painted as elitists who refuse to leave the comfy confines of the ivory towers, when in reality, they are locked in the tower, held captive by the evil stepmother that is our current funding system. Those who place the blame on scientists are just out of touch with the realities of basic science research.[8]

Reframed this way, the ivory tower is not a haven, but a prison made necessary by the realities of research funding. Librarians bring a unique perspective to this conversation. Not tied to any particular discipline, librarians can maintain a big-picture perspective on the economics of scholarly communication. With one foot in the ivory tower, librarians can understand the real pressures scholars face, while also advocating for non-experts, like students, who must engage with expert research.

This advocacy role is even more important in light of the rhetorical reasons why scholars write as they do. In his 2003 book *Clueless in Academe*, Gerald Graff casts this reason in a particularly negative light. Like other critics, he recognizes that scholarly articles are written by scholars for scholars, and that journal publication is a necessary professional achievement—but he also contends that some scholars believe they must write exclusively for expert audiences. If an article is too accessible, this line of reasoning goes, it is less likely to be published or received well. Graff argues that these scholars—who may be insecure about their identities as experts—will intentionally leave out the definitions, context and explanations that would make the "so what" or "who cares" of their work more transparent to people who are not in their fields. While educated people may be able to read these articles, they will almost certainly miss the point of them.[9]

Intentionally writing to exclude non-experts is neither defensible nor practical, but it is also only part of the story. Knowledge construction in western culture depends on scholars having spaces and places where they can talk to peers struggling with the similar, complex ideas. Scholarly knowledge is created in communities; it is a social and communicative act. At the point of creation, out on the cutting-edge, where they are dealing with ideas that are new and complex, it is not reasonable for scholars to translate their every thought for general audiences. Sometimes, language is complicated because the ideas it describes are complicated. Sometimes the work is difficult to read because the ideas are difficult to understand. If we value that complexity, then we must allow for its expression. Giroux

(2011) suggests that those who call for clarity at the expense of nuance or complexity are hiding a deeper, ideological agenda:

> I believe that the appeal to "clarity" has become an ideological smokescreen that conceals how the notions of common sense and simplicity are mere excuses for rejecting complex ideas and the careful use of language as a marker of the educated mind.[10]

Giroux does not let academics off the hook, but he does require the public, our students, to share responsibility for understanding the complex ideas scholars have to communicate.

As librarians, this approach should be attractive. We are educators, but we are focused on more than classroom success. Teaching librarians are interested in creating lifelong learners, who have the skills and disposition to be informed, active citizens. This perspective, however, requires us to respect and understand the work scholars do and to respect and advocate for our students. As Barbara Fister argued in 2012:

> One of the reasons I bridle when publishers say everyone who needs research publications already has access to them (apart from its insulting ludicrousness) is that too often we settle for false assumptions about both our work and the intellectual curiosity of the public. The walls of our gardens assume there is a natural barrier between the way we academics think and what ordinary people care about. This, to me, is a way of proclaiming ourselves a special class of useless.[11]

Scholars have many reasons for using and producing scholarly information. While some work to solve real world problems and inform real world decisions, connecting with the public is not always a primary goal. Librarians bring a broader perspective—we collect and preserve the knowledge created by scholars while we also help our students develop the skills they need to contribute to society—knowing that most of our students will make those contributions in the world outside the academy. Collecting scholarly information with a belief that it is useless except to scholars is shortsighted and cynical. Librarians are uniquely positioned within the academy to help students make their own connections to scholarly knowledge creation.

Empowerment & Cognitive Development

Our jobs would be much easier if students would just believe that the sources librarians collect (and faculty assign) are valuable based on our say so, but they don't. Perhaps it is human nature to look back on students of the past with rose-colored glasses, but these sentiments, expressed by Elizabeth Winslow in 1931, suggest that students have always demanded that their teachers show, not tell, them the value of the material they teach:

> To begin with, students have changed in their attitude towards their own education. The college classroom is no longer the proverbial sanctuary of learning we have been accustomed to think it is. It dare not be. Modern students do not regard themselves as in any sense set apart. They have not come as those who are about to explore a mystery. They do not feel peculiarly privileged. Nor do they bring any homage of awe to their supposedly wiser masters.[12]

A quick look at the learning outcomes or goals colleges and universities define for their graduates shows that we are not in the business of teaching students to mindlessly accept authority, even academic authority. They include: self-directed learning, community engagement, reflection, leadership, global awareness, multicultural competence and, of course, critical thinking. We want to give our students the tools they need to make informed decisions for themselves—to figure out what they think, based on the best information they can access, and to communicate those thoughts effectively and widely.

It is important to remember, though, that these are the goals we have for our graduates. Most undergraduates do not have the knowledge or the skills to do these things without help—and this is very clear when we look at how they use scholarly books and articles. Most undergraduates lack the subject knowledge to read and understand these sources as a scholar would. Beyond this, and even more important, most undergraduates lack the epistemological understanding they would need to use these sources effectively.

There is a multitude of research, extending back decades, examining the impact of college on student development. First introduced in 1970, William Perry's influential model suggests that, developmentally, students move from a position of *duality*, through *multiplicity*, and finally into *commitment*. Duality suggests that there are two types of answers—right and wrong—and the student's job to discover which are right. Multiplicity recognizes that there are multiple answers or perspectives on complex topics, but at this stage students lack the ability to evaluate or distinguish between them, so they approach them all as equally valid. It is only in the commitment stage that students are able to evaluate new information, integrate it with their prior knowledge, and make meaning for themselves.[13]

Perry observed undergraduate students over a fifteen-year period in the 1950's and 1960's to develop his model. His sample was not representative, and his work has been revised and refined by a number of subsequent researchers, but it is still influential. In this context, it suggests that our students are not cognitively developed enough to fully appreciate and understand knowledge as something that is created, using evidence—and that all knowledge (or evidence) is not equally valid. These concepts are essential to appreciate the process and the products of scholarly research, but mastering them is something people do in college; it is not a skill set they have when they arrive.

Scholarly sources provide the building blocks for this type of knowledge creation, and they are themselves the products of these processes. However, expecting students brand-new to college to change the way they think about knowledge by simply exposing them to scholarly sources is not realistic. And faculty, who are themselves specialists, may not be the best people to show students how scholarly sources can be useful for generalists.

Most college students are not training for the researcher's life, and they may not need to use scholarly information like scholars do, but they do need the ability to parse complex answers to complicated problems; understand how and why authors use evidence to support their claims; and evaluate how persuasive they are. It is not enough to say "just leave the expert research to the experts, and someone, somewhere will filter it down to you." In our world, our students would be left vulnerable to deceit and to those with harmful agendas.

Evaluating expert information as a generalist is a scary thing. In 2009, Julian Sanchez argued that in many cases it is impossible for a non-expert to evaluate scientific information on its face. He builds a persuasive case that as an expert; he can fabricate information that will seem credible to an educated non-expert. Even more disturbing is his contention that it is easier for someone trying to deceive to be convincing than it is for someone who is legitimately trying to explain a complex idea without oversimplifying. Educated non-experts trying to navigate scholarly information have to find other means for evaluating this discourse; just reading the articles, books and blog posts themselves is not enough.[14]

As knowledgeable and skilled as most scholars are, they are not generalists. The methods and metrics they use to evaluate scholarly publications are those of experts, of fellow participants in a discourse. As peer-reviewers and editors, they play a role in shaping the unwritten rules of that discourse. They have developed expertise in a specific field, and they use that expertise to evaluate new information. When faced with a question or argument about a related field, they are frequently unwilling to comment—precisely because they cannot bring the same level of expertise to those questions. Librarians, on the other hand, are experts at navigating unfamiliar fields. When we sit at the reference desk, teach a general education class, or talk to faculty in our liaison departments, we are doing just that. This is not to denigrate librarians' own expertise, but to say that part of librarians' own expertise is figuring out how to jump in to an unfamiliar discourse and make sense of it.

> We have a better grasp than may faculty in the disciplines do
> of just how challenging it is to master several different ways of
> knowing in any one semester. We help students develop some
> all-purpose ways to approach any question, knowing that this
> will remain an important ability later in life.[15]

As Perry's model suggests, many students do not even realize that there are different "ways of knowing." In a single term, they may need to navigate several ways—today it might be a psychology study about cross-cultural communication; tomorrow, research into the benefits of green tea; and next week making sense of climate change. Even if the unwritten rules were written, no one can be an expert in everything.

Librarians also bring a long view into the classroom. Library instruction sessions are partially about helping students navigate a particular assignment, or succeed in a particular class; but librarians also have a strong commitment to lifelong learning. Learning that "I can only get an A on this paper if I use scholarly journal articles" does not demonstrate the value of these sources beyond the classroom. Librarians can ask a different set of questions:

> Will students look to research to inform their decisions and
> opinion after college, or will the well-established patterns of
> research that they have developed to succeed academically be-
> come irrelevant when they've turned in their last college assign-
> ments. When they need to make decisions about their lives and
> their values, when they need to make choices about the issues
> that will shape the communities we live in and the future of our
> badly damaged planet, will they seek authoritative evidence to
> inform their views?[16]

To help students use scholarly research in a meaningful way, however, librarians must be clear about how these sources are authentically useful to non-experts, and engage in conversations outside the library to ensure that students participate in learning experiences that demonstrate that value.

Building Authentic Bridges

Right now, it is fair to say that academic librarians have an ambivalent relationship towards our own scholarly discourse. Librarians straddle the line between practitioner and scholar; many active professionals do not publish at all in traditional books and journals. Even among the subset of librarians who work in academic libraries, there is a perception that those who publish only do so to meet the requirements of tenure.[17] In Hardesty and Sugarman's study about the professional literature some librarians indicated that they use books and journals to stay informed professionally. For others, though, these were not important resources. Timeliness was one factor working against these sources for some; the length (and writing style) of the articles was another. Some came right out and said most of this literature is "dull and uninspired," or "of dubious value and quality."[18]

While Hardesty and Sugarman were specifically examining the impact of technology on the professional discourse in librarianship, the problems they point to have been around for much longer than blogs and Twitter. In 1999, Fisher's review of the professional literature in librarianship concluded that "[a] synopsis of how our professional literature is depicted leads us to believe that most of what makes its way into print is not very good.[19] Fisher also suggests why this dissatisfaction may exist, and the reason mirrors the scholar/practitioner divide. Librarians expect many things from their professional discourse: rigorous research that provides a theoretical basis for our work, as well as practical accounts that can inform our day-to-day decisions:

> Perhaps one of our problems has been that many of our journal publications try to deal with both of these concerns simultaneously. So the reader looking for rigorous research reports is satisfied with only part of a journal's contents, and the practitioner looking for the "how we done it good" article is also only partially satisfied with the contents of a journal.[20]

The problems that exist within the library literature are far beyond the scope of this essay, but librarians' uneasy relationship with this literature is important. When librarians use the scholarly literature to inform our own practice, and when we conduct scholarly research to inform our practice, we can develop models for using scholarly research that will be useful to our students. When librarians dismiss the literature in librarianship as useless, this can have important ramifications. Too often, librarians arguing for changes in undergraduate learning take the real barriers standing between undergraduates and scholarly sources to mean that these sources will be irrelevant after college—which is why Barbara Fister's example is so important. She has engaged in scholarly communication, understands the economics of scholarly communication, and can passionately and authentically argue for its value. When she argues (with librarians, with writing faculty, with audiences across academic disciplines) that forcing students to write research papers from scholarly sources before they are ready to understand those sources teaches the wrong lessons, it is not because she does not believe these sources are valuable, or because she believes only scholars can appreciate that value.

Nowhere is this clearer than in her frequent discussions of the traditional first-year "research paper." In these conversations, she blows past a question we have spent a great deal of time discussing—"How can we help students write better research papers?"—and cuts directly to the more important and interesting—"What do we want students to gain from research paper assignments?" Increasingly, Barbara Fister concludes that we are fixing the wrong problems:

> When we teach argument from sources, we tend to get hung up on the fiddly bits: how the library works and how to cite sources correctly and avoid plagiarism. When we focus on what kind of how many sources must be included, we forget that our students may not have the patience and skill required to read and understand much of what they find.[21]

Instead of focusing on these "fiddly bits," we should teach students to write from sources using the sources they are ready to use; which, in many cases, are the most appropriate sources for the types of arguments they are making. When students are required to use sources they are not ready to use meaningfully, they learn to check off requirements, pull out quotes without understanding them, and find other ways to "fake it."[22]

Instead, she argues that we should develop assignments that help students develop skills they need to create knowledge:

> ..if you want first-year college students to understand what sources are for and why they matter, if you want them to develop curiosity and respect for evidence, your best bet is to start by tossing that generic research paper.[23]

The values articulated here are notable because they are a librarian's values, representing the profession's goals and values. Curiosity, inquiry, and respect for sources and evidence: these are values shared across the academy, but they are particularly important to librarians.

Librarians value exploration, lifelong learning, and the ability to use sources to learn and to make decisions as a primary goal. Our partners in the disciplines value these things too, but in different ways, as they usually focus on the knowledge contained within their discipline. Librarians are free to think about how students can apply these skills across the disciplines, inside and outside the academy. Faculty in the disciplines use research papers as a way to assess what students have learned about a particular subject, or topic. The ability to craft an argument is important, but they do not have the freedom to reward a cleverly constructed argument built on a mistaken understanding of the subject. Librarians can focus on the journey.

And when traditional assignments, like the three-peer-reviewed-articles research paper, do not help students understand how scholarly research and expert information will help them in the "real world," librarians need to make the case, broadly and loudly, for learning experiences that will be more relevant. Librarians need to work from the assumption that our students are curious and capable of appreciating the sources we collect and the research we support. When we assume that scholarly sources are only valuable to scholars, then the ivory tower becomes the cloister it is traditionally compared to. When that happens, this safe space is at its most vulnerable.

Why is this Important?

What will be lost if public support for research and inquiry disappears? A great deal. When the world of scholarship is seen as wholly separate from the "real world," the assumption grows that the work that happens within the ivory tower could never survive outside of its boundaries. To a certain extent, this assumption is true, as the market determines what kinds of research and inquiry have immediate commercial value, and private dollars tend to go where that value exists. However, it does not follow that those things that cannot survive in a market-driven world *should* not survive at all.

It's seductive to see the market as a reliable arbiter of value and significance; it can have a simplicity that seems objective and transparent. As a result, those who defend science and inquiry frequently accept the underlying premise that it is economic benefit (and fairly immediate economic benefit) that makes research and inquiry important. This narrative usually sounds like this: a researcher may not have the immediate intention to produce a commercially viable application, but lots of important discoveries have been made by accident, by researchers engaged in basic research about how the world works. Therefore, it is important that researchers engage in inquiry even when they cannot anticipate (profitable) discoveries like penicillin, or Viagra, or the Internet.

In fact, the idea that "basic research" is necessary because it will eventually support commercially or strategically important discoveries provides the underpinning for the way research and inquiry is organized and funded in the United States, particularly in science and technology fields. Reaching back seven decades to Vannevar Bush's influential *Report to the President*, which lays out the justification for public support for research, one can find this thread:

> Basic research leads to new knowledge. It provides scientific capital. It creates the fund from which the practical applications of knowledge must be drawn. New products and new processes do not appear full-grown. They are founded on new principles and new conceptions, which in turn are painstakingly developed by research in the purest realms of science.[24]

Bush's vision goes beyond the "accidental discovery" narrative. He argues that the way we "do science" relies is dependent upon on the constant accumulation of new knowledge. Federal money should support this knowledge accumulation, and higher education provides a safe space, where scientists and experts can conduct research "relatively free from the adverse pressure of convention, prejudice or commercial necessity.[25]

As convincing as this narrative is, relying on market (or military) value to generate support for inquiry is dangerous. The market will never protect all forms of inquiry, as some questions are not commercially important to answer, and some questions lead to "wrong" (or potentially costly) answers. There are entire disciplines, topics and methods of inquiry that have never and probably will never hold widespread interest or appeal.

In the last year, these limitations have been brought into vivid relief as the infrastructure Bush envisioned has come under attack. In 2012, the House of Representatives passed the Flake Amendment, which proposed to significantly change how the National Science Foundation dispenses research dollars. The NSF currently provides funding for research in the social sciences, including political science, but the Flake amendment would divert all funds currently going to political science research (about $9 million) to research in the natural and physical sciences. By passing this amendment, the House of Representatives made a political statement about what kind of research is valuable, and what kind is not.[26]

In a widely discussed opinion piece in the *Washington Post*, Charles Lane argued that "Flake's amendment does not go far enough: the NSF shouldn't fund *any* social science."[27] In this article, and a follow-up, Lane contends that research in the social sciences should not be publicly funded because these disciplines do not lend themselves to definitive, clear, answers: "the 'larger' the social or political issue, the more difficult it is to illuminate definitively through the methods of 'hard science.'"[28] If there is value to these softer questions, he continues, the market will reflect that: "If this [political science] research is as valuable as its proponents say, someone other than the U.S. Treasury will pay for it."[29] The editors of *Nature* magazine decried Lane's attempt to "constrain political scientists with utilitarian bean-counting" as antithetical to "the free academic nature of the whole exercise."

It is useful at this point to return to the metaphor of the ivory tower. The ivory tower has represented a place where pure inquiry, unsullied by outside concerns and agendas, can happen. Traditionally, free inquiry has been at the heart of the academic enterprise,[30] but today that idea is complicated, as outside agendas have influence within the ivory tower. In the middle of the twentieth century, research money poured into American colleges and universities via channels like the National Science Foundation. Even private institutions not directly dependent upon public monies became dependent on these indirect sources of public funding, and reward structures within the university began to reflect the university's new values.[31]

Federal money is not the only source of influence within the ivory tower. To illustrate this, we can turn to another political and media flashpoint from 2012: the unsuccessful effort by the Board of Regents at the University of Virginia to forcibly remove University President Theresa Sullivan. The specific point of conflict here was online education, but it is the influence wielded by large private donors that is relevant to this conversation. When public support for higher education recedes, donors with deep pockets can demand influential positions (like those on the UVA Board of Regents). This has long been the case, but as universities increasingly depend on those donations to deliver core services, donors also expect that any and all demands they make will be met. UVA law professor Siva

Vaidhyanathan points out that while most donors want to serve the public interest, some have other agendas:

> So too often an institution that is supposed to set its priorities based on the needs of a state or the needs of the planet instead alters its profile and curriculum to reflect the whims of the wealthy. Fortunately, this does not happen often, and the vast majority of donors simply want to give back to the institutions that gave them so much. They ask nothing in return and admire the work we do. But it happens often enough to significantly undermine any sense of democratic accountability for public institutions.[32]

While Vaidhyanathan focuses on public institutions, this story is just as relevant to private institutions that have long relied on donor support.

In its response to the Flake amendment, the editorial team at *Nature* magazine asked, "Should public opinion help to decide which areas of science are studied or funded?"[33] The reality is, though, that public opinion *will* play a role in these decisions. This has obvious and direct implications when it comes to taxpayer-supported funding for research, but it is increasingly true in the university environment as well. Only a general public that understands the value of inquiry—and the ways that it supports knowledge creation—will support research, and by extension, higher education. This means that non-academics need to have more nuanced and complete understandings of what kinds work is being done in our laboratories and libraries.

So, while we may want to reply to attacks on the scholarly enterprise by protesting that "we *are* doing things that benefit society!"; or by decrying public "interference" in funding, these responses will not protect open inquiry. Public opinion does have a place in this story, and librarians believe that scholarship and inquiry are public values. They are the fundamental reasons why we do what we do.

Conclusion

There are two sides to the metaphor of the ivory tower. On the one hand, it evokes privilege and irrelevance; it represents a space where a chosen few are distanced from real world problems. On the other hand, the ivory tower allows and supports free inquiry; it is a place where knowledge is pursued for its own sake, and where learning more about the world, and about ourselves, is valued.

Librarians are uniquely positioned to fight the negative aspects, and protect the things worth protecting in the ivory tower, but to do so, *we must get out of the library*. When we behave as if the scholarship we support, and the materials we collect, are only valuable within the academy, we lose our chance to create support for the work we do outside the walls of the ivory tower.

> *"In the past Wisdom might dwell in an ivory tower aloof from direct interest in actual life, a kind of umpire of its issues. But that is no longer possible, if only because the very value of Wisdom itself is in debate, and it must defend its tower"*
>
> ~Joseph Fort Newton
> *Atlantic Monthly*
> December 1929

NOTES

1. Anon., "Ivory Tower," OED Online. Oxford University Press (2012), http://www.oed.com/view/Entry/100387?redirectedFrom=ivory=tower.
2. Barbara Fister, "Undergraduates in the Library," Blog. Library Babel Fish, http:www.insidehighered.com/blogs/library_babel_fish/undergraduates_in_the_library_trying_not_to_drown.
3. ———, "Open and Shut: a Case for Preparing Our Students for What's Next," Blog, Library Babel Fish, http://www.insidehighered.com/library-babel-fish/open-and-shut-case-preparing-our-students-what%E2%80%99s-next.
4. Henry Giroux, *Education and the Crisis of Public Values: Challenging the Assault on Teachers, Students, and Public Education*, [New York: Peter Lang, 2011].
5. Christie Wilcox, "Guest Editorial: It's Time to e-Volve: Taking Responsibility for Science Communication in a Digital Age" The Biological Bulletin, 222, no. 2 (April 1, 2012) : 85-87.
6. Kate Pratt, "Reaching Out: Science as a PR Problem," Blog Soapboxscience, http://blogs.nature.com/soapboxscience/2012/05/30/reaching-out-science-has-a-problem.
7. Richard Demillo, "Abelard to Apple: The Fate of American Colleges and Universities." [Cambridge, MA: MIT Press, 2011.]

8. Jeanne Garb, "Reaching Out: Why are Scientists Trapped in the Ivory Tower and What Can Be Done to Escape?," Blog, Soapboxscience, http://blogs.nature.com/soapbox-science/2012/05/31/reaching-out-why-are-scientists-trapped-in-the-ivory-tower-and-what-can-be-done-to-escape.

9. Gerald Graff, "Clueless in Academe: How Schooling Obscures the Life of the Mind. [New Haven, CT: Yale University Press, 2003.]

10. Henry Giroux, "Education and the Crisis of Public Values: Challenging the Assault on Teachers, Students, and Public Education, [New York: Peter Lang, 2011, 100.]

11. Barbara Fister, "Serial Scholarship: Blogging as Traditional Academic Practice," Blog, Library Babel Fish, http://www.insidehighered.com/blogs/library-babel-fish/serial-scholarship-blogging-traditional-academic-practice.

12. Elizabeth Winslow, "New Models in Scholars: How Different are the 1931 Products?," The North American Review, November 1930: 598.

13. William Perry and Harvard University Bureau of Study Counsel, "Forms of Intellectual and Ethical Development in the College Years: A Scheme, Holt, Rineholt, and Winston, 1970.

14. Julian Sanchez. 2009, "Climate Change and Argumentative Fallacies," Blog. Julian Sanchez, http://www. Juliansanchez.com/2009/04/06/climate-change-and-argumentative-fallacies/.

15. Barbara Fister. 2011, "Information Literacy: Undervalued and Ubiquitous?." Blog, Peer to Peer Review, http://www.libraryjournal.com./lj/home/8930770264/information_literacy_undervalued_or_ubiquitous.html.csp.

16. Barbara Fister, 2010, "Truth or Dare," Blog. Peer to Peer Review, http://www.libraryjournal.com/lj/communityacademiclibraries/887643-419/truth_or_dare__peer.html.csp.

17. Skye Hardesty and Tammy Sugarman, "Academic Librarians, Professional Literature, and New Technologies: A Survey" The Journal of Academic Librarianship, 33, no. 2 (March 2007) : 195-205; William Fisher, "When Write is Wrong: Is All our Professional Literature on the Same Page?" Library Collections, Acquisitions, and Technical Services, (1999) 23, no. 1: 61-72.

18. Skye Hardesty and Tammy Sugarman, "Academic Librarians, Professional Literature, and New Technologies: A Survey" The Journal of Academic Librarianship, 33, no. 2 (March 2007) : 195-105.

19. William Fisher, "When Write is Wrong: Is All our Professional Literature on the Same Page?" Library Collections, Acquisitions, and Technical Services, (1999) 23, no. 1: 61-72.

20. William Fisher, "When Write is Wrong: Is All our Professional Literature on the Same Page?" Library Collections, Acquisitions, and Technical Services, (1999) 23, no. 1: 61-72., 70.

21. Barbara Fister. 2012, "Taking the Long View with First Year Writers," Blog, Library Babel Fish, http://www.insidehighered.com/blogs/library-babel-fish/taking-long-view-first-year-writers.

22. Ibid.

23. Barbara Fister. 2011, "Why the 'Research Paper' Isn't Working," Blog. Library Babel Fish, http://www.insidehighered.com/blogs/library_babel_fish/why_the_research_paper_isn_t_working.

24. Vannevar Bush. 1945, "Science the Endless Frontier: A Report to the President by Vannevar Bush, Director of the Office of Scientific Research and Development." U.S. Government Printing Office. Washington D.C., http://www.nsf.gov/od/lpa/nsf50/vbush1945.htm.

25. Vannevar Bush. 1945, "Science the Endless Frontier: A Report to the President by Van-

nevar Bush, Director of the Office of Scientific Research and Development." U.S. Government Printing Office. Washington D.C., http://www.nsf.gov/od/lpa/nsf50/vbush1945. htm.

26.   Mervis, Jeffrey, and Jane J. Lee. 2012. "House Takes Pot Shots at Research and Ocean Policy." Blog. *ScienceInsider*. http://news.sciencemag.org/scienceinsider/2012/05/house-takes-pot-shots-at-research.html.

27.   Charles Lane. 2012. "Congress Should Cut Funding for Political Science Research." The Washington Post, June 5, sec. Opinion.

28.   Charles Lane. 2012, "Congress Should Cut Funding for Political Science Research." The Washington Post, June 5,sec. Opinion.

29.   Ibid.

30.   Ehrlich, Thomas. 1995. *The Courage to Inquire: Ideals and Realities in Higher Education*. Bloomington: Indiana University Press.

31.   Richard DeMillo, Abelard to Apple: The Fate of American Colleges and Universities. [Cambridge, MA: MIT Press 2011, 8.]

32.   Siva Vaidyananthan, "Strategic Mumblespeak, Slate, June 15, 2012 http://www.slate. com/articles/news_and_politics/hey_wait_a_minute/2012/06/teresa_sullivan_fired_from_uva_what_happens_when_universities_are_run_by_robber_barons_.html

33.   Anon., "A Different Agenda," Nature 487 (7407) (July 19, 2012): 271.

REFERENCES

Anon. 2012a. "Ivory Tower." *OED Online*. Oxford University Press. http://www.oed.com/view/Entry/100387?redirectedFrom=ivory+tower.

———. 2012b. "A Different Agenda." *Nature* 487 (7407) (July 19): 271–271. doi:10.1038/487271a.

Bush, Vannevar. 1945. *Science the Endless Frontier: A Report to the President by Vannevar Bush, Director of the Office of Scientific Research and Development*. U.S. Government Printing Office. Washington, D.C.: U.S. Office of Scientific Research and Development. http://www.nsf. gov/od/lpa/nsf50/vbush1945.htm.

DeMillo, Richard A. 2011. *Abelard to Apple: The Fate of American Colleges and Universities*. MIT Press.

Ehrlich, Thomas. 1995. *The Courage to Inquire: Ideals and Realities in Higher Education*. Bloomington: Indiana University Press.

Fisher, William. 1999. "When Write Is Wrong: Is All Our Professional Literature on the Same Page?" *Library Collections, Acquisitions, and Technical Services* 23 (1): 61–72. doi:10.1016/S1464-9055(98)00126-2.

Fister, Barbara. 2010a. "Undergraduates in the Library, Trying Not to Drown." Blog. *Library Babel Fish*. http://www.insidehighered.com/blogs/library_babel_fish/undergraduates_in_the_library_trying_not_to_drown.

———. 2010b. "Truth or Dare." Blog. *Peer to Peer Review*. http://www.libraryjournal.com/lj/communityacademiclibraries/887643-419/truth_or_dare__peer.html.csp.

———. 2011a. "Why the 'Research Paper' Isn't Working." Blog. *Library Babel Fish*. http://www. insidehighered.com/blogs/library_babel_fish/why_the_research_paper_isn_t_working.

———. 2011b. "Information Literacy: Undervalued or Ubiquitous?" Blog. *Peer to Peer Review*. http://www.libraryjournal.com/lj/home/893077-264/information_literacy_undervalued_or_ubiquitous.html.csp.

———. 2012a. "Taking the Long View with First Year Writers." Blog. *Library Babel Fish*. http://

www.insidehighered.com/blogs/library-babel-fish/taking-long-view-first-year-writers.
————. 2012b. "Open and Shut: A Case for Preparing Our Students for What's Next." Blog. *Library Babel Fish*. http://www.insidehighered.com/blogs/library-babel-fish/open-and-shut-case-preparing-our-students-what%E2%80%99s-next.
————. 2012c. "Serial Scholarship: Blogging as Traditional Academic Practice." Blog. *Library Babel Fish*. http://www.insidehighered.com/blogs/library-babel-fish/serial-scholarship-blogging-traditional-academic-practice.
Giroux, Henry A. 2011. *Education and the Crisis of Public Values: Challenging the Assault on Teachers, Students, & Public Education*. Peter Lang.
Hardesty, Skye, and Tammy Sugarman. 2007. "Academic Librarians, Professional Literature, and New Technologies: A Survey." *The Journal of Academic Librarianship* 33 (2) (March): 196–205. doi:10.1016/j.acalib.2006.12.006.
Lane, Charles. 2012a. "Congress Should Cut Funding for Political Science Research." *The Washington Post*, June 5, sec. Opinions. http://www.washingtonpost.com/opinions/congress-should-cut-funding-for-political-science-research/2012/06/04/gJQAuAJMEV_story.html.
————. 2012b. "The Academic Hornet's Nest." *The Washington Post - Blogs*. http://www.washingtonpost.com/blogs/post-partisan/post/the-academic-hornets-nest/2012/06/13/gJQALJhYaV_blog.html.
Mervis, Jeffrey, and Jane J. Lee. 2012. "House Takes Pot Shots at Research and Ocean Policy." Blog. *ScienceInsider*. http://news.sciencemag.org/scienceinsider/2012/05/house-takes-pot-shots-at-research.html.
Perry, William Graves, and Harvard University Bureau of Study Counsel. 1970. *Forms of Intellectual and Ethical Development in the College Years: a Scheme*. Holt, Rinehart and Winston.
Pratt, Kate. 2012. "Reaching Out: Science as a PR Problem." Blog. *Soapboxscience*. http://blogs.nature.com/soapboxscience/2012/05/30/reaching-out-science-has-a-pr-problem.
Sanchez, Julian. 2009. "Climate Change and Argumentative Fallacies." Blog. *Julian Sanchez*. http://www.juliansanchez.com/2009/04/06/climate-change-and-argumentative-fallacies/.
Vaidhyanathan, Siva. 2012. "Strategic Mumblespeak." *Slate*, June 15. http://www.slate.com/articles/news_and_politics/hey_wait_a_minute/2012/06/teresa_sullivan_fired_from_uva_what_happens_when_universities_are_run_by_robber_barons_.html.
Wilcox, Christie. 2012. "Guest Editorial: It's Time To e-Volve: Taking Responsibility for Science Communication in a Digital Age." *The Biological Bulletin* 222 (2) (April 1): 85–87.
Winslow, Elizabeth. 1930. "New Models in Scholars: How Different Are the 1931 Products?" *The North American Review*, November.

Section III

Publishing and the Academic Library

E-books: The Future of Our Readership?

Rebecca Hamlett
Instruction and Archive Librarian, Charles F. Curry Library, William Jewell College

William Jewell College is a small, private, liberal arts college in the Kansas City, Missouri metropolitan area, with a full-time enrollment of approximately 1,100 students. The traditional four-year residential college was founded in 1849, and the current library, Charles. F. Curry Library, was built in 1964. In 2001 this library has held approximately 250,000 print volumes of periodicals, books, and archival materials. In 2011, the college, as part of a fundraising campaign, received a $1 million challenge grant from the J.E. and L.E. Mabee Foundation to assist with fundraising for a new facility, the Pryor Learning Commons. The Mabee Foundation provides grants to a variety of non-profit institutions of higher learning in six states, including Missouri. Major gifts were contributed to the project by Juanita Trotter, the Pryor family, the Hall Family Foundation, William T. Kemper Foundation, the Sunderland Foundation, JE Dunn Construction Company and the Gary Dickinson Family Charitable Foundation. The Pryor Learning Commons project is part of the vision of the college to move the institution into the 21st century learning environment to accommodate the learning styles of today's students. The new learning commons includes spaces that have been designed to promote collaboration, innovation, and active learning opportunities. The $15 million funding goal for the new learning commons was met in early 2012, and the construction project began in May, 2012.

Curry Library has traditionally been considered the "intellectual center of campus."[1] Its three-story building holds the library's print collection, a 24/7 accessible computer lab, circulation services, and other academic library services. It also allows students access to technology such as printing, scanning, and photocopying. However, many changes are anticipated with the advent of the Pryor Learning Commons, scheduled to open in August, 2013. The new 25,000 square-foot facility will house facilities that were not available in the library, such as digital classrooms, presentation studios, video conference rooms, 3D printers, and training labs. Library staff will also have newly-designed offices.

In preparation for the new Pryor Learning Commons, the print collection was relocated two floors below its previous location. This new area is smaller, so a collection redevelopment plan was created, based on criteria established by the library director. Most print periodicals published prior to 1970 were withdrawn to make space for the print books. The library director estimates that the library has reduced the print collection over the last few years to approximately 105,000 items. As construction began on the college's quad, the library building was remodeled to house college administration offices on the second floor, which had held most of the library's print materials. Student services offices were moved to the first floor, which had housed the student study areas and the library offices. Pending completion of the new learning commons, professional librarians and paraprofessional library staff moved to temporary offices.

The library currently employs three professional librarians and two paraprofessional staff. There is a library director, systems librarian, and instruction/archive librarian, and the full-time paraprofessional positions include a daytime circulation supervisor and an evening circulation supervisor. The library also employs an average of 33 student workers in the spring and fall semesters, who work an average of six to eight hours per week. After construction, the print circulation duties will remain in the building with the print collection while the other circulation and professional staff will relocate to the new Pryor Learning Commons. Additionally, open hours for the general stacks—where all print books and periodicals are held—will likely be reduced. Because most patrons will find the collection to be less accessible, this new configuration presents one of the biggest challenges created by the learning commons.

Prior to the building initiative, access to digital and print materials had been only adequate. For example, there was not a detailed collection development plan for library acquisitions; print materials were purchased when faculty members requested titles to support research and coursework. Consequently, holdings across disciplines were quite uneven; some subject areas had robust and cutting-edge materials, and others were out-of-date or obsolete. And, while the library's database subscriptions had been sufficient to support curricular goals, the staff was constantly evaluating their electronic resources, and trying to keep up with technological advances and new products. The posts of systems librarian and the instruction librarian, who were to be responsible for essential library tasks and additional technological responsibilities, were created to address some of these issues.

Moving toward a Digital Library

In early 2011, the library director made a much more radical, and potentially trend-setting, choice—William Jewell would eliminate the print materials budget for one year, with the exception of a small number of critical print periodicals. This decision was met with skepticism by some faculty members, while others embraced the change. One interesting observation by the instruction librarian was that in some cases these reactions seemed at times to be discipline-specific. While the nursing department relies on the latest research and focuses heavily on electronic journals, some members of the history and music departments emphasize print materials, including historical manuscripts and printed music scores. The library staff evaluated the current electronic databases utilizing quantitative and statistical data to ensure the academic disciplines of campus departments were met. For example, the library purchased a subscription to the Library Music Source database which includes over 35,000 music scores that can be downloaded and printed. Digital resources were to become the focus of the library's budget and services, with an emphasis on making technological offerings current and improving access points. The library contracted with Serials Solutions for the Summon Discovery Service; added larger multidisciplinary databases, such as ProQuest Central; and upgraded from Academic Search Premier to Academic Search Complete.

The decision to primarily focus on e-books to supplement the library's print collection was also made in February 2011. Faculty members were still encouraged to request critical titles for purchase, and the library director reviewed these requests. However, librarians strongly encouraged patrons to use interlibrary loan to request print items that were not critical to the curriculum. If a requested item was available in digital text, it was purchased in that format. And when faculty members specifically requested items in print format, they had to justify why they wanted the text instead of the electronic version. When electronic versions were unavailable, or significantly more expensive, print versions were purchased for the collection.

Before March 2011, the library purchased digital texts through what was NetLibrary, which is now owned by EBSCO, and held approximately 4,300 titles through the platform. Although the library staff wanted to reduce the number of platforms, NetLibrary was kept by the library staff because of the investment made through the purchase of the titles. Nevertheless, the NetLibrary platform was unpopular, and many patrons found it difficult to use. New users, especially, did not like the platform. And college librarians did not want to purchase additional titles at list prices (as required by NetLibrary) and wished to explore additional subscription options. Hoping that NetLibrary's low usage was more reflective of the service itself, and not e-books in general, the staff began to explore additional e-book vendors.

Ebrary, with the Academic Complete collection, was one of the newer e-book vendors evaluated by the library staff. A free trial of the service was obtained, and other academic libraries seemed to be moving in the direction of ebrary. Cost was also a factor; the library director was able to purchase the subscription at a discount because of the packaged purchase price of ebrary, ProQuest Central, and Summon. After experiencing the trial, the librarians made the decision to subscribe to the collection based on cost analysis, its user-friendly platform, and available titles. The main drawback to a subscription service was that it did not offer opportunities for librarians to select individual titles within the purchase price of the Academic Complete collection. The collection included titles chosen by ebrary, and there were no a la carte selections without having to purchase additional titles at list price in addition to the collection. However, ebrary could quickly add 70,000 titles in academic subjects, and supplement the print collection. Titles could also be purchased for multi-user access at 150 percent of list price, which the librarians felt was extremely reasonable. Instead of purchasing multiple copies of one title for more than one person to access at a single given time, the multi-user option allows for many users to access the title at the same time while only spending an additional one-half of the purchase price. After the service was successfully tested by the librarians, and then by faculty members, it was implemented in May, 2011.

Marketing efforts helped librarians implement ebrary at the college; the vendor provided posters and other promotional materials, and emails about the service were sent to faculty and students. In August 2011, demonstrations were conducted during faculty workshops and additional instructions were shared with faculty. The instruction librarian strongly promoted the service to students during one-time instruction sessions, which are usually held in the fall semester. After the Machine-Readable Cataloging (MARC) records were uploaded into the catalog, the titles were available via the electronic link on the library's proxy server. And by the spring of 2012, electronic texts accounted for almost fifty percent of William Jewell's library books.

Currently, the ebrary Academic Complete collection includes more than 78,000 titles from hundreds of publishers, including many prominent university presses, for academic librarians to choose from.[2] All titles have been published since 2000; one-third of the collection has been published in the last five years; and new titles and publishers are consistently added. The library is also taking advantage of the Data Sharing Fast (DASH) product, which is a digital institutional repository that is hosted on ebrary's servers and is accessible through ebrary's online platform. The library is digitizing students' Honors Projects, interdisciplinary scholarship compiled for more than forty years, which will be uploaded and searchable with ebrary's Optical Character Recognition software. And the library can choose to include digital repository records in the Online Public Access Catalog, or restrict access to authorized ebrary users.

But there are drawbacks to the service. Library staff does not have the ability to personalize the Academic Complete package to the college's curricular needs; ebrary chooses the titles that are included in the package, and substitutions cannot be made. While this has allowed the librarians to focus on the maintaining the remaining print collection, ebrary includes titles and subject areas that do not always match our disciplines. Some faculty members have told library staff that many available titles simply do not seem relevant. For example, the collection offers 776 anthropology titles, but William Jewell does not offer anthropology courses. While the college boasts a strong psychology program, ebrary offers only 990 titles in this subject area.

Faculty are encouraged to replace print textbooks through ebrary's multi-user access program, but there has been some resistance to electronic text use by faculty and students, perhaps because some traditional textbooks are not available through ebrary. As of August 2012 librarians had only supplemented the Academic Complete collection with one title and had not yet used the patron-driven acquisition options or short-term lending models. And, although the multi-user feature was attractive to the library staff in its review of e-book platforms, only two such titles had been purchased. In addition, multi-user titles are not always available for purchasing and availability is at the discretion of the publisher.

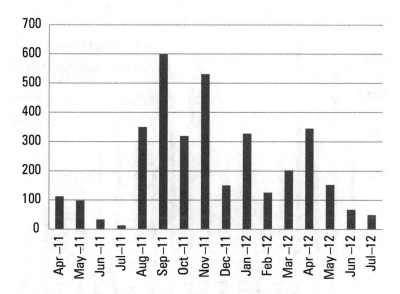

Figure 8.1. Ebrary Titles Checked out by Month

Figure 8.1 represents patron use of the Academic Complete collection. Although library staff was concerned that the electronic format would not be well received, the results have been more than satisfactory. From April 2011 to July 2012, 1,629 unique ebrary titles have been accessed a total of 3,472 instances. Since the service has been in place at the library for just more than a year, including the trial and implementation period, statistics are shown for the entire subscription period for descriptive purposes. We noted that usage sharply fluctuated after initial marketing and education efforts. The statistics may also show fluctuation in spring of 2012 based on student assignments.

The usage statistics are comparable with the print materials that have checked out from the library's general collection of print materials (figure 8.2). From April 2011 to July 2012, there were 8,317 titles checked out from the general collection by William Jewell College patrons, which includes all circulating print books. By July 2012, there were approximately 110,000 print materials held in the General Stacks, compared with the 78,000 ebrary electronic texts. The fluctuation of the electronic texts ac-

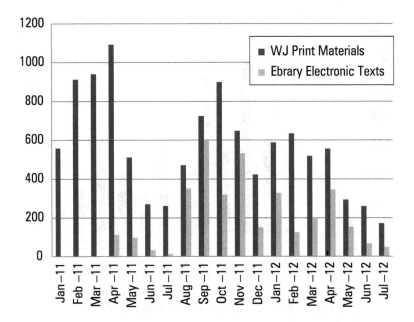

Figure 8.2. Total Checkouts of Circulating Library Materials by Format

cessed mirrors that of the print collection, with some variance. In addition, the data indicates that circulation of print materials has been decreasing.

In November 2011, at its highest point, the checkout of ebrary electronic texts accounted for 45 percent of the library's total circulation (figure 8.3). At its lowest point after implementation and minimal patron education, July 2011, electronic texts still accounted for approximately 16 percent of total circulation. These percentages suggest that library staff can consider ebrary an asset in meetings patrons' needs. Nevertheless, librarians wish to boost e-text usage through education, marketing, and collection development.

Transition Challenges

The majority of the students who attend William Jewell College are between the ages of 18 and 22 years old. In the fall of 2012, the instruction librarian informally polled students during library instruction courses, and found that only two out of ten students had ever read an e-book. Some students said they were disinterested in digital format, others said they did not know how to access e-books. Some William Jewell College students also expressed a preference for print books. Similarly, in a 2010 study, surveying undergraduate and graduate students at Sam Houston State University, 10.5 percent of students said they owned an e-reader device, while 44.7 percent said they "had no interest in owning an e-reader."[3]

The library circulation supervisor at William Jewell's library had some relevant patron encounters. For example, one student asked her about checking out a specific book. The circulation supervisor advised him that the library only had the title in digital format, which could be immediately accessed and downloaded using library e-readers, the student said he would prefer a print copy. Even after being informed that the only way the library could obtain a print copy was through interlibrary loan, which could take up to 10 days, the student opted for the print copy. A number of times during this transition year at the college, even when students were comfortable asking for help with library services they would choose print ma-

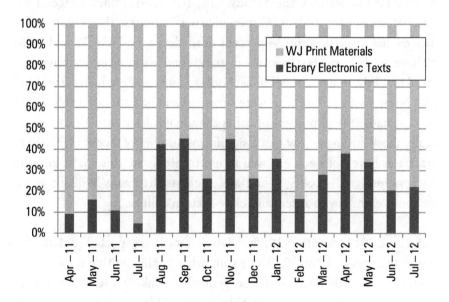

Figure 8.3. Percentage of Print and Electronic Materials
Accounting for All Circulation

terials even when there was a considerable wait for them. This student said he preferred to read print books, and referred to them, as some students encountered did, as "real books." Nevertheless, once students were shown how to access e-texts through ebrary and the library website, they became much more receptive to digital resources.

The instruction librarian also noted other unexpected deterrent to e-text use: requirements regarding citations in research papers. The three main predominant styles used at William Jewell College are the guides published by the American Psychological Association, Modern, Language Association, and University of Chicago. These stylebooks have quickly adapted to electronic publishing formats, and do not always provide clear guidance. So, students and faculty members were relieved to learn that electronic books can be cited just like print books—the style is exactly the same—and they are becoming more comfortable using them in their research.

A 2012 Pew Research Center study, "The rise of e-reading," suggests additional reasons for student inexperience with e-books. The Pew study indicates that, overall, some 34 percent of readers aged 18 to 29 and 30 to 49 have used e-texts. But there are disparities once formal education is factored in. Only 19 percent of high school students and graduates have read an e-book. Out of those who were surveyed and had attended college, 34 percent had; and 35 percent of college graduates have read e-texts. Once again, these findings show that a significant number of recent high school graduates have not been exposed to electronic texts. This study, and the observations of the college librarians, suggests that many William Jewell students learn how to access and use e-texts in college.

Before the 2012 transition, William Jewell librarians expected students between the ages of 18 and 21 to be somewhat familiar with e-books. They assumed that millennials would be, generally speaking, more receptive to digital formats and learning than older patrons.[4] However, they are discovering that this may not be the case. The 2012 Pew study, reported that only

21 percent of Americans have read an e-book in the previous year, even as reading of e-texts is increasing.[5] Thus, it is critical that librarians and faculty support positive initial experiences with electronic texts, as these interactions may influence lasting perceptions of the format. And it seems most effective for one-time instruction sessions to be offered to first-year students at William Jewell College. Librarians also plan to expand information literacy efforts, and improve instruction on how to access and use electronic texts, especially as the library continues to increase its e-text holdings and the new learning commons is launched. The Commons will house computer terminals, where students and faculty can access electronic materials and tools.

A noteworthy exception to the instruction librarian's informal polling was students in the Accelerated Nursing Track (AT) program at William Jewell College. Participants in the AT program are required to have completed their undergraduate degrees and other prerequisites, and go through a rigorous application process. Students who meet these requirements can complete their Bachelor of Science in Nursing in 12 or 16 months. While the ages of these students vary widely, most are employed full-time in medicine, and seem to have some basic familiarity with electronic databases and research. When these students were separately polled, the instruction librarian found that an average of 6 out of 10 students had read an e-book. And these students were very excited about "incentives" to encourage e-book use, and the library's subscription to Overdrive.

Listening to Patrons

In the summer of 2012 the library implemented new incentives to encourage patrons to use electronic texts. Before the transition, the library had leased popular (and non-academic) print books through McNaughton's book lease service. For a price, the library could request and receive a limited number of titles from McNaughton, and for two months, the books would circulate to William Jewell College library patrons. Then, the cataloging librarian would return the books, and choose new bestsellers to lease. This very popular service was eliminated in 2010, because of budget cuts. But in January 2012, William Jewell's librarians began to explore options to replace this service, and also encourage the reading of e-texts.

Again, the librarians relied on their own experiences and the literature; for example, the 2012 Pew study reported that 80 percent of e-book readers read for pleasure. They decided to subscribe to the Overdrive service, which two public library systems in the Kansas City Metro Area had already utilized. Unlike McNaughton, these titles were purchased outright. The Mid-Continent Public Library system, comprised of 30 branches in the metro area, and the Kansas City Public Library system, with ten branches, holds thousands of electronic titles with multiple copies. New titles are offered for purchase from Overdrive and its participating publishers on a regular basis, and at this time the Mid-Continent Public Library offers almost 12,000 electronic titles. Because some William Jewell College library patrons patronized one or both of the public library systems, it was hoped that the new interface would be familiar to some users.

The library director allocated $2,000 for the initial purchase of titles for the collection. Staff chose titles based on personal and patron preferences, and certain criteria: they would not purchase HarperCollins titles because of the publisher's cap on loans, 26 maximum per title; and they would not purchase audio books. (To date, the library director has only purchased three audiobooks—each installment in *The Hunger Games* series—that were not available as e-books at the time of release). In February 2012, 104 single-user titles were put in circulation, and the library staff was trained on the platform. Three additional orders were placed between February and May, bringing the library's Overdrive collection to 189 titles.

Between February 2012 and July 2012, patrons checked out 80 unique titles (figure 8.4). These titles circulated 172 times. While many titles have only circulated once, 21 titles have circulated three times or more. (The title with the highest circulation statistic at this time, unsurprisingly, is *Fifty Shades of Grey*, the first book in the *Fifty Shades Trilogy* by E. L. James, with 11 checkouts.) Because more than 42 percent of the purchased titles have

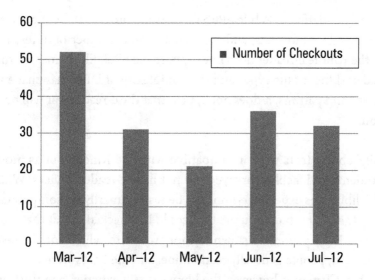

Figure 8.4. Total Circulation of Overdrive Titles

circulated in less than six months, the library staff feels confident about increasing the number of Overdrive titles. Patrons have been encouraged to suggest additional titles for purchase, and librarians will continue to solicit their ideas as new orders are placed.

Evaluating E-Readers and Other Devices

As new technology continues to emerge that enables patrons to access electronic texts in a digital format, the library staff continues to explore additional options for making texts accessible to patrons. Much of the discussion revolves around technology, compatibility, and Digital Rights Management (DRM). With DRM, the texts purchased in an electronic format cannot be downloaded or read on unauthorized platforms, and cannot be shared between individuals or institutions in the same way that inter-library loan books are shared. The publisher determines on which platforms and as what file types the texts can be read. The library staff was initially hesitant to subscribe to or purchase multiple formats of materials because of the ambiguous future of electronic text formats. For example, a Kindle text can only be read on Kindle e-reader devices, but it can also be read on tablets if a Kindle app is installed. An iBook can only be accessed on an Apple platform. While ePub formats are proving to be the forerunner of digital text formats, and are readable on a number of different devices, the Kindle e-reader does not support the ePub file format. With the myriad of different file types and the complexity of DRM has challenged librarians and patrons, it does not appear that the e-reader war will be easily won.

Initially, ebrary texts were incompatible with the Kindle, but as most of the students and faculty surveyed did not have e-reader devices, William Jewell's librarians expected e-books to be read primarily on computers, including three laptop computers that could be checked out at the circulation desk. Ebrary offered its own e-reader software, which could be easily downloaded, people generally read offline, and the PDFs were universally accessible. Currently, however, the library is still experiencing frustration with ebrary and mobile devices. The library utilizes a proxy server which restricts access to authorized users with a library card for online library services, and because of the proxy server and firewall, at this time library users must log in to the ebrary service using a facebook account on mobile devices. The library staff is yet to find a work-around for this process, but hopes that ebrary will improve its access for access methods such as this.

In summer of 2011, several developments allowed patrons access to additional formats. Apple released the second generation of iPads, and more importantly, the college received a grant to purchase new iPads for all faculty members. In effect, the college had chosen a side in the tablet wars, and faculty were encouraged to utilize this new technology in their courses. Fortunately, new formats and apps—including Adobe Digital Editions, iBooks, the Kindle app, Evernote and BlueFire Reader—were available on the iPad. The iPad allowed patrons to access Kindle e-books, iBooks, and Overdrive texts, in addition to PDF journal articles through the library's database subscriptions, all on one device. Tablets proved to be much more versatile than traditional e-reader devices and faculty were enthusiastic about exploring the numerous apps available that provided access to online resources. In addition, the librarians saw an increase in tablet ownership by students, although with slower growth because the students were responsible for their own purchase of the devices.

In the fall of 2011, librarians also decided to purchase three fourth-generation Kindles to test their reception and usage by faculty and students. As they could not afford to purchase iPads for the library, the library's staff hoped that the e-readers would allow them to try out checkout procedures, authorization methods, and gauge patron interest. Supplemental readings, selected by the English department, were uploaded to the Kindles. Many of these titles were classical works, out of copyright and freely available, so cost was minimal. Checkout procedures were devised, and each device was linked to the library's Amazon account; this would allow students to download titles using their own Amazon accounts. These downloads would be removed when staff checked the devices back in, but the library's downloads would remain. These Kindles were made available for an initial checkout period of one week at the circulation desk.

There they sat. And as of August 2012, almost a year later, there had been no circulation of the devices. The staff concluded that one reason for patron disinterest was the lack of a substantial marketing plan. When purchasing and implementing new products, the librarians generally incorporated promotional pushes, tied to normal academic cycles: faculty workshops are held in mid-August; student orientations are scheduled at the beginning of September; and student instruction takes place, primarily, in the first eight weeks of the fall semester. Because the Kindles were not purchased until September 2011 and title downloads took much longer than anticipated, the fall semester was well underway and the marketing window had narrowed considerably.

The Kindles were also not integrated into the one-time instruction sessions facilitated by the instruction librarian, largely because of time constraints; typically, the librarian has 50-60 minutes to conduct the session. There was not a great deal of time to review critical library services and new products—including a new Discovery database service and other large databases—had to be included. Consequently, e-reader instruction was not a high priority during these sessions. Additionally, ebrary—the main service providing e-texts in the library—made Kindle use more cumbersome and time-consuming, as it only allows one chapter or 60 pages to be downloaded for offline reading.

Furthermore, by early 2012 William Jewell librarians began to suspect that the fourth- generation Kindle was simply obsolete. The lack of a touchscreen was a major disadvantage; the Kindle's black and white screen competed with tablets that were quickly becoming affordable, including the iPad, which all faculty members owned. Ebrary texts are fully available on the iPad for those that are willing to log in with their facebook logon information, and most students were satisfied to access ebrary texts on their computers; many still do not own tablets or other e-reader devices. When the Kindle Touch was released, it offered a touchscreen many patrons now expect on mobile devices, and the Kindle Fire offered more functionality than the fourth-generation Kindle. So when the library's Kindles were marketed directly to students at the circulation desk, a frequent response was, "That's all it does?"

However, members of the library staff still believe an e-reader lending program is feasible and desirable. In November 2012 William Jewell's librarians attended a workshop session led by Mary Anne Mercante, Assistant Dean at Maryville University in St. Louis, Missouri, and Julie Portman, Technical Services Librarian at Fontbonne University in St. Louis, Missouri. William Jewell's full-time enrollment is slightly higher than either of these institutions, but each had implemented successful e-reader lending programs in the previous year. Both schools offered three versions of the Nook, and two versions of the Kindle. In addition, Fontbonne had purchased two Kindle Fire devices, and Maryville offered the Kindle Fire, the Nook Tablet, the iPad, and the Samsung Galaxy. The libraries had acquired an Amazon Prime account for patron use; this allowed additional content to be viewed through the library's account. Full marketing plans were implemented at both institutions, and they were effective. By the summer of

2012, Fonbonne's e-reader devices and tablets had circulated a total of 170 times. Maryville's circulation was comparable, with 168 total checkouts.

These and other examples suggested to William Jewell's librarians that they should move forward with new library device lending plans. The Systems Librarian intends to purchase additional devices in the fall of 2013 including those purchased by Fontbonne and Maryville, However, the challenge of technological advances continues. The systems librarian is exploring the purchase of iPads for checkout at the new learning commons, but at the same time Android-based tablets are becoming much more affordable. The question becomes whether the library staff should wait to see what the latest devices will be or be resigned to the fact that there will always be new devices and begin a program based on the current technology.

Choosing devices is more complicated because of access models and software applications are rapidly changing. Popular titles are still purchased through Overdrive, because staff did not believe Amazon was a sustainable option for electronic texts when this choice was made. Furthermore, Amazon allows an account to be used on, up to, five devices; the library account could only be authorized for access on three library Kindles and two other devices, the director's and the circulation desk's computers. These limits on access were not attractive to the library staff.

However vendor models are changing and the Kindle format is becoming more flexible. For example, Amazon recently decided that Amazon Prime customers could choose up to one title per month from more than 145,000 books in the Kindle owners' lending library; the library could borrow as many books as Amazon accounts held, and librarians already anticipate creating additional accounts as new Kindle devices are purchased. So, for the flat cost of $79 per year, the library could access to titles without purchase. Amazon also offers free Prime accounts to students, and they could sign into their own Amazon accounts and independently download books. The Prime Instant Video service—with an Instant Video App available on Kindle, Apple, Android, and multiple platforms—is a bonus that will be attractive to students.

Furthermore, Amazon users are able to lend select titles to other Amazon account holders. (Publishers and rights holders determine which titles are eligible for lending.) A borrowed title can be used on devices that support Kindle's reading app. While Amazon only enables books to be lent just once, there are additional websites such as Lendle.me and ebookfling.com that circumvent this restriction for owned titles.

Conclusion

Librarians are riding the waves of technological change, along with everyone else. Digital texts and electronic resources offer librarians and patrons new ways to access information, and include functionality and new opportunities for collaboration. Patrons benefit from targeted instruction about library services and new technology, but librarians must also market these features to emphasize the value of digital materials. To facilitate marketing and promotion, librarians must continue self-education efforts through research and hands on experience with these tools. The digital world is changing rapidly, and new models that enhance use and applicability of e-texts are emerging. William Jewell's librarians have made mistakes during this meaningful transition period, but they have also gathered valuable information about the behaviors and needs of their patrons.

This information will allow them to better evaluate future vendors and models, and help improve the success rates of future programs and initiatives. Ideally, librarians should be able to focus on creating information sessions for new e-text users; the goal should not be to necessarily replace print materials, but to supplement the holdings of the library's book collection in the most easily accessible and appropriate formats possible to support patrons' needs. With the opening of the new Pryor Learning Commons in the fall of 2013, the librarians at William Jewell College anticipate expanding the library's e-book collection through additional vendors. The focus on e-books has been successful and while the library director focuses on a strong marketing plan to accompany the new Pryor Learning Commons, the instruction librarian plans to emphasize access methods and ease of use in the library instruction sessions and through additional online tutorials. The librarians believe that they are moving in the right direction to provide patrons with tools to succeed in the 21st century learning environment. It is an exciting time in the field of library and information science in higher education, and William Jewell College librarians will always pursue and leverage technological advances to boost access and engagement with information.

NOTES

1. William Jewell College, "Library: Contact Us," August 3, 2012, http://www.jewell.edu/librarycontact.us.
2. Ebrary, "Subscription Database Title Preview: Academic Complete," http://www.Ebrary.com/lib/academiccompletetitles/home/action.
3. E.D. Cassidy, G.G. Britsch, T. Manolovitz, L. Shen, and L. Turney, "Higher Education and Emerging Technologies: Student Usage, Preferences, and Lessons for Library Services" Reference and User Services Quarterly, 50, no. 4 : 380-91.
4. K. Zickurh, K. Purcell, K. Madden, J. Brenner, "The Rise of E-Reading" Pew Research Center's Internet and American Life Project, http://libraries.pewinternet.org/2012/04/04/the-rise-of-e-reading/.
5. Ibid.

The Burning Barn:
Transparency and Privacy in e-Science and e-Health

P. F. Anderson
Emerging Technologies Librarian, Taubman Health Sciences Library, University of Michigan

Introduction

> *"Emerging at our conscious doors"*
> ~Thomas Merton

Barbara Fister has always been able to identify and discuss emerging issues, trends, and concerns in librarianship, and foreground them in her writings and professional dialogues. When asked to contribute to this volume, Barbara's treatment of transparency and openness leapt out at me. Two of her recent blog posts published on *Inside Higher Ed* were of particular interest: "The Value of Doing Research—and Sharing It" and "I'm Not Buying It: The Importance of Privacy for Research."[1,2]

Superficially, these two posts seem to present similar opinions. In "The Value of Doing Research—and Sharing It," Barbara argues persuasively about disjunctures between tenure criteria; the quality of academic scholarship; measures of scholarly productivity; and the economics of intellectual property rights. She expresses her concerns pointedly in the following statement:

When knowledge is created primarily to advance individual careers and corporate profits, yet is by design limited to those who can pay for access, we're not advancing knowledge. We're just creating property that we trade for personal recognition.[3]

To emphasize her argument, she restates this in plain language.

What I am saying is that scholars who feel pressure to publish when they have nothing compelling to say shouldn't be forced to do so, and publishers shouldn't be given the job of deciding who gets tenure. This procedure supports a system that once made research available but now (because of the volume and the cost) makes our research inaccessible to most people. That's tragic.[4]

Tragic, indeed, and Barbara's assessment is supported by most in the profession, and many in the ranks of academic research. Barbara brings her inimitable depth and subtlety to this conversation, as always. The 2012 Elsevier boycott, with over twelve thousand academics refusing to participate in Elsevier journals, brought public attention to the current publishing model, and how it creates barriers to appropriate and fair access to information [The Cost of Knowledge: http://thecostofknowledge.com]. She continues with additional arguments in favor of sharing. In this context, sharing means public sharing (such as publishing in open access venues) or personal sharing (such as faculty who model critical thinking, research skills, and the delights of discovery with students.) Barbara holds models of effective research in high esteem, especially when entire academic communities benefit. While there is not a direct plea for engagement with social media, that could be inferred from the number of blog posts cited and praised in the same discussions as frustrations with fee-based barriers to quality content.

The title "I'm Not Buying It: The Importance of Privacy for Research" could be interpreted as an extension of these arguments, with Fister implying that privacy is not critical for research, and possibly detrimental. This position is gaining ground and finding followers within the Open Science movement. It is central to translational science, the increasingly urgent effort to rapidly move new research findings into clinical practice. It is even more central to the "open laboratory" and "open notebook science" movements, both of which reveal information about new science in progress before the research findings are publishable. However, that is not what Barbara was saying in that essay, rather the reverse:

> One bit of library capital that hasn't been borrowed by social media companies is our respect for privacy as a condition fundamental to intellectual freedom. We don't want to look over your shoulder when you read. We don't want to provide information about what you're reading to others.[5]

Barbara argues persuasively, but briefly, against the "filter bubble"[6] and in favor of her "belief that the search for knowledge should be fundamentally different than shopping." The implication of these two essays when juxtaposed is that the right to personal privacy in certain situations is as foundational to the process of discovery as is sharing in other circumstances.

> Research is, by its nature, social. We build on one another's ideas and we share ours publicly to keep the conversation going. But it's not social the way Facebook is.[7]

The public dialog in science and healthcare around these topics often focuses on a linear dynamic, with transparency and privacy as opposing factors. Proponents of each stance vigorously oppose the alternative, each arguing risks and dangers. Barbara has opened the door to a more nuanced view of this dialog. It is this I'd like to explore.

Before "Transparency" and "Translation"

"And drink these deeps of invisible light."
~Merton

I vividly recall one event that illustrated a turning point towards increased transparency in science. At the annual meeting of the International Association for Dental Research in 2005, National Institutes of Health (NIH) Director Elias Zerhouni presented an early morning keynote. The audience was a bit sparse in the large, dark hall. These presentations were usually like annual updates, detailing the funding of great discoveries, and featuring slides with words and diagrams. Deans at research universities, lab directors, and corporate research and development managers paid close attention at these functions. Few expected that Zerhouni would propose a critical shift in research priorities, with new concepts and new terms. Halfway through his talk, I had shifted from taking dutiful notes to frantic typing, and felt stupid because I did not understand the terms he was using. After his presentation finished, I was stunned. Outside the lecture hall, I was quickly surrounded by research faculty from the University of Michigan, my institution, with others joining the crowd. Everyone had the same question, which Renny Franceschi, our Associate Dean of Research, urgently articulated: "What is translational science? What does it mean?" I was flattered they thought the librarian would know, but I was as baffled as they were. Zerhouni's seminal article on this "invisible light" that would penetrate life science organizations and journals would not be published for another six months.[8] I replied, over and over, "I don't know, but I'll find out." When finally published, Zerhouni opened his article with this statement:

> It is the responsibility of those of us involved in today's biomed-
> ical research enterprise to translate the remarkable scientific in-
> novations we are witnessing into health gains for the nation.[9]

That was the "translational" part of translational science. He outlined several challenges, from the exponential growth of the published literature in science and research (with the annual number of articles added to MEDLINE jumping from just over 300,000 in 1996 to over 600,000 ten years later to divisions between disciplines that impair discovery and use of discoveries.[10] He also addressed the most important impediment to translating research into practice.

> At no other time has the need for a robust, bidirectional infor-
> mation flow between basic and translational scientists been so
> necessary.[11]

He perceived the "siloing" of researchers, as individuals and as communities in tightly focused disciplines, as a limit to communicating across boundaries. This obstacle to information and opportunities results in fractures and knowledge loss, and creates unnecessary and dangerous gaps. A solution to an urgent problem might emerge completely outside of the discipline focusing on the challenge.

The Rewards of Boundary Spanning

Boundary spanning was not an entirely new idea to me. In graduate school at the University of Michigan, my mentor Maurita Holland directed me to Thomas J. Allen's work on technological gatekeepers in engineering research and development.[12] Allen revealed the dangers and costs of closed communication systems, as well as motivations for systems to close.

> The employing organization cannot afford (or believes it cannot afford) to allow free communication between its members and people outside of the organization. In an attempt to protect its proprietary interests the organization erects barriers to prevent the transmission of its research results to the world at large. This attempt to stem the outward flow of information cannot help but affect inward flow as well.[13]

Similarly, this research highlighted strong correlations between performance and productivity and the ability to span boundaries, and connect information sources through person-to-person networking.

> There existed in the organizations that they studied, a small number of key people upon whom others relied very heavily for information. These key people, or "technological gatekeepers," differ from their colleagues in their orientation toward outside information sources. ... They also maintain broader ranging and longer term relationships with technologists outside of their organizations. The technological gatekeeper mediates between his organizational colleagues and the world outside, and he effectively couples the organization to scientific and technological activity in the world at large.[14]

The core idea was that boundary spanning and interconnectedness spurs growth and innovation for individuals and organizations. Allen distilled this succinctly: "The gatekeepers were outstanding performers. The liaisons were average. Now the isolates appear as very poor performers."[15]

Studies on technological gatekeepers persists to this day, and this research has yielded efforts to transform communication patterns in many kinds of organizations, even in healthcare.[16,17] For these organizations, the research may be forming the foundation of translational science. Indeed, the gatekeeping literature is tightly coupled, through citation networks and practice, to the literatures on the invisible college[18,19] and organizational decentralization.[20] Invisible colleges can be considered a precursor or subset of another field, social network analysis. Translational science and social network analysis provide strategies to study communication patterns and develop more flexible, agile, responsive, dynamic, and innovative organizations.

The Costs of Knowledge Gaps

Riding the train back from an American Society for Information Science meeting in 1988, Don Swanson chatted with me about his vision of new library research, to discover and expose previously undiscovered connections between academic disciplines.[21] In Swanson's seminal work in this area, he exposed connections between the peripheral circulation problems associated with Raynaud's Syndrome and dietary fish oil, which was known to increase peripheral vascular circulation, Don published an article on how fish oil might be potential therapeutic agent for Raynaud's in 1986, and in 1989 a clinical trial was published validating the idea.[22]

In 1988, Don was seeking other examples of knowledge gaps, and had found one: how magnesium might be used treat migraines.[23,24] In 1989, major clinical studies were published proposing a connection[25,26] and these cited Don's paper. In the early 1990s, several reports were published, and the first multicenter clinical trial was released in 1994.[27,28] By the mid-1990s, magnesium was being used in clinical trials.[29] In 1998, magnesium was mentioned as a possible exploratory treatment in clinical reviews.[30] In 2012, magnesium was finally included in two clinical guidelines, one on migraine treatment[31] and another on migraine prevention.[32]

I know several people treated for migraines, based on information derived from Don's discoveries, including one young boy who suffered for several years from severe and debilitating migraines. Before a specialty clinic discovered his magnesium deficiency, there were series of scary misdiagnoses, hospital visits, large quantities of risky medications with horrid side effects, years of school absences, and accusations of faking it to get attention. That discovery made a profound shift in the quality of life for that young man and his family. He was being treated with magnesium several years before it was recommended in guidelines, and because of that intervention, he was able to turn around his academic record. I cannot help but imagine what might have happened to that child if Don Swanson had not written his article on magnesium precisely when he did.

Qualifiers, Subtleties, Shifts, & Distinctions
Morris, Wooding, and Grant explore how time lags delay adoptions of discoveries, showing how this is a primary driver of translational science in their 2011 study. They strongly assert the "speedy translation of research into practice is a good thing." They were able address this premise by developing a model to estimate the economic benefits of cardiovascular disease (CVD) research.

> One recent study (of which JG and SW were co-authors) estimating the economic benefit of cardiovascular disease (CVD) research in the UK between 1975 and 2005, found an internal rate of return (IRR) of CVD research of 39%. In other words, a £1.00 investment in public/charitable CVD research produced a stream of benefits equivalent to earning £0.39 per year in perpetuity. Of this, 9% was attributable to the benefit from health improvements, which is the focus of this paper. (The remaining 30% arise from 'spillovers' benefiting the wider economy.) This level of benefit was calculated using an estimated lag of 17 years.[33]

That excerpt refers to the 2008 Rand Health Economics Research Group report, "Research: What's it Worth?" which clearly articulated assumptions about returns on investment (ROI) in medical research. You will notice immediately that most estimated benefits are indirect in the report, and estimates were made of the time to assess benefits. Their 2011 paper attempts to clarify the relationship between ROI; the length of time required to show a positive ROI; and measures used to assess benefits. Since most measures relate to funding processes and peer-review publications, the metrics used to determine time lags depend on the grant and publication lifecycles.

> For example, the gap between guideline publication and translation into actual practice is often ignored, suggesting an underestimation of the time lags in some cases. On the other hand, interventions may come into use before guidelines outlining them have been published—suggesting an overestimation of time lags in other cases.[34]

The gist of their findings comes down to this: We don't know any of those things—not ROI, not the economic value of research, not the impact of time lags to adoption. More importantly, we might be looking at the question of measuring the value of research backward.

> There is a clear trend in the literature to seek a single answer to a single question through the calculation of an average. The variation found in the literature suggests that this is not possible (or even desirable), and variation matters.[35]

There is a strong belief among research community leaders that openness, transparency, sharing, and collaboration lead to better research and faster discoveries, but we have not figured out how to prove this assertion, nor do we know if faster research is always better.

> It also perhaps requires stakeholders to develop a more nuanced understanding of when time lags are good or bad, linked to policy choices around ethics and governance for example, or reflect workforce issues.[36]

David Brin, the famous science fiction author and physicist, examines how these principles inform research, and society at large.

> What has worked—the foundation of our liberties—has always been openness and candor. Especially the ability to force the mighty out in the open where we can hold them accountable. All three of the greatest human inventions—science, democracy and free markets—depend on open information flows.[37]

Focusing more specifically, Brin explains the challenging attitudes toward transparency in science, and the important roles played by scientists who are pushing for transparency.

> Whenever I have given public talks about transparency, I found that certain types of audiences react differently.... But my most difficult audiences by far are scientists. When I speak in praise of criticism as an antidote to error, they shrug.[38]

From Brin's perspective, the current emphasis on transparency has been spurred by the internet and related innovations. He describes how the internet's origins set the stage for our current direction.

> It came from science. Scientists conceived it, built it, improved it, and then shared it with everybody, all according to the principles the live and work by. In its nascent forms, the Internet had little use for encryption or anonymity, because these were alien concepts, anathema to most of its originators. Rather, it burgeoned, thrived, and grew beautiful in an ambience of near-total accountability.[39]

In 2005, the push was on to open the silos in science and foster increased dialog, sharing, and collaboration. The NIH Public Access Mandate[40] required that publicly funded research be published in publicly accessible journals, giving researchers and the public access to quality information. More grants were made to support collaborative projects, open sharing of data, and boundary-spanning communications between teams and organizations. Explicit efforts were made to share data and discoveries between basic life science researchers (working in labs, often at the "bench") and clinical researchers (working with patients at the "bedside"), with a goal of fostering awareness in primary care providers of the newest discoveries in patient care research.

This concept is at the heart of "bench-to-bedside" work, although use of the phrase dates back to the mid-1980s,[41] long before "translational science" came into common usage. "Bench-to-bedside" is falling out of use because it underemphasized "bidirectionality," with "bedside-to-bench"[42] and "research-to-reality"[43] or "molecule to marketplace" substituted for it. It is absolutely essential for bench researchers to listen to clinical researchers and patients.

> When you think about it, it's really starting with the patient. So sometimes you're focusing your work with the patients, and sometimes you have to go to the laboratory and do some very basic science experiments, but the goal is always to bring it back to the patient. So the name has been changed to Bedside-to-Bench.[44]

Patients also need to be regarded as full partners to increase communication speed about data quantity and quality.

Most translational science efforts focus on integrating the work of academic and industry scientists, and they leave out a critical set of participants: patients. This is problematic because the speed and quality of the feedback between the bench and the bedside is a critical rate-limiting factor for medical progress. Two groups have come to the conclusion that breakthroughs in translational medicine require collecting data on patients, including outcomes, on a scale never previously attempted and making those data available with appropriate privacy protections to translational researchers.[45]

Science Made Social, Data Made Huge

> *"And heaven, in floods, comes pouring in"*
> ~Merton

Another powerful effort supporting collaboration between the public, scientists, and clinicians is active recruitment of patient representatives by the Cochrane Collaboration for systematic review teams.[46] The Cochrane Collaboration is the largest and most authoritative publisher of evidence-based reviews on health care, for clinicians and consumers. They actively engage the public in both reviewing evidence and translating evidence into lay terms.

> Cochrane review authors may consider questions for review because of their own interests and experiences as clinicians or healthcare researchers. These are not always the questions that are of most concern to healthcare consumers and their families and careers.[47]

Science 2.0, citizen science, participative science, open science, open notebook science, collaborative scientific discovery, science of team science, and crowdsourcing are just a few of the buzzwords dominating trends in science methodologies, revealing the public's new engagement with research and healthcare. Non-academic engagement in science ranges across contributing data or specimens; contributing brainpower or other resources; contributing financial support through crowd funding; to writing for growing online and open science communities. More and more scholarly publications—including some of the most prestigious and influential publications—list authors who are not academics.

The National Audubon Society (NAS) Christmas Bird Count is the oldest and longest-running citizen science survey, with their 113th annual count ending on January 5, 2013.[48] In 2010, the count included more than two thousand community bird watching groups, with tens of thousands of individuals gathering data that is then collected, compiled, organized, and analyzed, before being published as the annual publication, American Birds.[49] Recently, NAS made changes to incorporate trends in citizen science and lowered barriers to entry for potential citizen scientists, and expanded the activities available to participants. The data is used not solely by the organization, but informs government policy development and implementation, and contributes to other research on climate and environmental change.

> Data from the Audubon Christmas Bird Count are at the heart of hundreds peer-reviewed scientific studies and inform decisions by the U.S. Fish and Wildlife Service, the Department of the Interior, and the EPA. Because birds are early indicators of environmental threats to habitats we share, this is a vital survey of North America and, increasingly, the Western Hemisphere.[50]

In the Audubon study, citizen scientists make contributions of labor, time, and data. The data is initially compiled by local organizations, and then transferred to the national organization for further compilation and analysis. In this project, individual participants are not typically acknowledged beyond expressions of gratitude for the collective effort. This is a marvelous example of a top-down citizen science effort, driven primarily by the needs of the science in partnership with the interests of the citizen participants.

One of the most fascinating stories of discovery emerged from Galaxy Zoo, the great granddaddy of citizen science initiatives. Galaxy Zoo, established a successful citizen science model followed by other projects, from those focused on outer space to those researching deep oceans to translate papyrus, whale songs, and other incredible projects. The Galaxy Zoo model allows the public to analyze scientific data through training, gaming, and community. The most influential discovery from the original Galaxy Zoo efforts has come to be called Hanny's Voorwerp.[51]

I first heard the story of the origins of Galaxy Zoo, and the discovery of Hanny's Voorwerp, at Pamela Gay's 2009 presentation in the Meta Institute for Computational Astrophysics (MICA) lecture series in Second Life.[52] Second Life is a 3D online virtual world that provides opportunities for research and citizen science projects, in addition to educational events like the MICA lecture series, which is significant enough to be partially archived through APOD (Astronomy Picture of the Day).[53] Pamela described the Galaxy Zoo background, arising from the imagination of an overworked graduate student in 2007;[54] the development of the game interface; and content reviews by community forums with professional oversight. The overworked graduate student was faced with a big data problem—a million deep space images that needed to be classified, and more were coming. One day, a week after joining Galaxy Zoo, a primary school teacher noticed an object which puzzled her so much she returned to the image after clicking past it, and began to ask questions about it in the community forums.

Hanny's Voorwerp, a glowing green shape that resembles Kermit the Frog, is now thought to be galaxy-sized clouds glowing with remnants of light from a quasar that no longer exists, having collapsed into a massive black hole. The object has been named after the Dutch schoolteacher who found it, Hanny van Arkel, and "Voorwerp," Dutch for "object" or "thing."[55] Note that Hanny is one of many Galaxy Zoo volunteers. Galaxy Zoo community forums were essential to this discovery, and acknowledged in the published article. For example, "This publication has been made possible by the participation of more than 100,000 volunteers in the Galaxy Zoo project. Their contributions are individually acknowledged at http://www. galaxyzoo.org/Volunteers.aspx."[56]

Online, the Galaxy Zoo model has been applied to other topic projects under the umbrella organization Zooniverse, as well as other initiatives such as FoldIt, famous for gamers solving in three weeks an HIV genetic puzzle that had frustrated scientists for years.[57,58,59] These examples, and hundreds of others, justify these comments of Phil Plait on the potential impact on science of the public: "It doesn't always take a degree, or years of training, to make an impact on science. All it takes is interest. That can lead to love, and a degree, and training… or just to more interest. But clearly, that can be enough."[60]

As with the first Hanny's Voorwerp article, FoldIt included some of the gamers as authors in the official publication. Because of the size of the groups, teams were listed, rather than individuals in the teams. We see this often in clinical guideline publications; an international collaboration team might be listed in the author credits, along with a handful of individuals who led the project. Alternatively, publications can also lit each individual involved with a project. A 2012 article on the discovery of the Higgs-Boson particle was five pages long, but the list of authors and their affiliations ran for twelve pages.[61] This style of providing attribution stirs complaints about accountability, as it's more difficult to determine who did what on each project. Jaime da Silva highlights failings of current models for attribution, such as ICJME guidelines, urging more flexibility (and accuracy) in reporting.[62] It is clear that this is an area in flux, with solutions yet to be discovered.

A different collaborative research model are drug discovery efforts to find new malaria treatments through open access, public domain, and something resembling Creative Commons licensing. This is more of collaborative science, rather than citizen science, such as the Medicines for Malaria Venture (MMV) that began providing the Open Access Malaria Box in December 2011[63] in association with the Drugs for Neglected Diseases *initiative* (DNDi). The Open Access Malaria Box delivered 400 compound solutions with suspected antimalarial activity to more than 100 scientists in 20 countries. The selection of compounds derived from searches of the public domain literature, with all recipients required to publish any new data from their research also in the public domain. The searchable data archive for MMV is in ChEMBL, a database of "bioactive drug-like small molecules." The project's individual components (papers, blogs, etc.) are hosted in an open Smart Research Framework via LabTrove at the University of Southampton, which also houses data, diagrams, PDFs, and associated files. For discussion and promotion of the project, extends through social media, including Facebook, Twitter, Google+, YouTube, forums, and wikis.[64]

The MMV also makes use of a variety of online academic social spaces. Their OpenWetware wiki collects the current partners, divisions of labor, along with information on materials, protocols, and other resources.[65] The group uses Mendeley, a tool that combines bibliographic management with academic social networking, where they have collected almost 100 articles about the MMV initiative. The MMV website has links to over 200 publications and reports of the collaborative, and one article provides an overview of the discoveries and best practices of the group.[66] The efforts are open to anyone who is interested and able to contribute. Still, even with the strong presence online and in social media sites, open MMV's primary contributors and partners are trained scientists publishing in peer-reviewed journals, making this effort similar to a traditional research process.

Part of the power of social media and open science communities is in the increased potential to include voices that are excluded from dominant publication models, and hierarchical structures in academia and corporations. There are many stories of quirky folk with discoveries who did not "fit in" or initiatives that did not fit the current paradigm being excluded from publication. My favorite story of this sort is of Garrett Lisi, a particle physicist who did not feel comfortable in academia or corporate environments. After earning his Ph.D. in particle physics, he moved to Hawaii and became a surfing instructor. However, he was not forced to completely give up his love of particle physics. He joined a niche social network online and focused on his interests, blogged, and made friends through social media. He proposed one idea that his online friends urged him to publish. With their support, on November 6, 2007, he posted the article to the Arkiv, a pre-publication service for the hard sciences.[67] Just a week later, on November 14th, he made international news with an article in the British newspaper titled "Surfer dude stuns physicists with theory of everything."[68]

When I met him in Second Life a couple years later, I asked him about the amazing rapidity with which his obscure and highly technical article received such attention. Lisi chuckled, and said simply, "My peeps." The people, his friends, believed in him and his ideas, and made certain they received attention. Garrett has gone on to give TED talks, many presentations, and time has been allotted on the Large Hadron Collider to test his theory. Even twenty years ago, it would have been unthinkable for a "surfer dude" to achieve such renown in a discipline like physics without a supporting institutional framework.

Lisi's friends ensured his quirky brilliance was not excluded from the scientific record. The Medicines for Malaria Venture fosters open high-level collaborations between scientists and scientific teams seeking ways to treat an overlooked disease. FoldIt used gaming and a SETI-like approach to sharing human brain power in search of solving a complex pattern recognition problem. Galaxy Zoo used gaming and communities to address the challenges of overwhelmingly large datasets. And the Audubon's Christmas Bird Count partners with hobbyists—acknowledging their personal passion for birding—to gather data that could not gathered by trained scientists. There are many more problems and solutions, but the sheer range and diversity of this tiny sample hopefully illustrates the need to explore these types of collaborations, and preserve information about them.

Personalized Medicine & the Quantified Self vs. HIPAA?

> *"It is not yet the grey and frosty time*
> *When barns ride out of the night like ships"*
> ~Merton

Big data challenges are not limited to the hard sciences; they are present in virtually every discipline. The good news for hard scientists is that they do not have to worry about a galaxy, for example, getting upset about a photo posted on Facebook. But in the health sciences, there are special types of big data challenges, compounded by complicated ethical issues. The use of collaboration technologies and tools to generate big data present unique and complex rewards and risks, with evolving challenges, processes, and policies.

Across the US, there is fairly widespread awareness of the Health Insurance Portability and Accountability Act of 1996, better known as

HIPAA.[69] Perhaps less well-known are the Patient Safety and Quality Improvement Act of 2005 (PSQIA)[70] and the Clinical Laboratory Improvement Amendments (CLIA) of 1988, which has had several updates and revisions. Each modifies the HIPAA privacy requirements for handling, managing, and creating health information for patients and healthcare organizations. To simplify, PSQIA focuses on patient safety as it relates to privacy, while CLIA provides patient access to laboratory results without physician permission. The Affordable Care Act (ACA) of 2010[71] potentially impacts privacy, and some have expressed concerns about the government having full access to medical records.[72] The health industry has also shared about the Physician Payments Sunshine Act (section 6002 of the Affordable Care Act), requiring doctors to divulge their major donors. This directs attention to the question of informed consent and potential bias or influence on treatment and care choices. Not being a lawyer, I will not attempt to go into the actual guidelines, but will focus more on how they are perceived and some of the impacts on behavior and potential consequences for information flow.

There is a perception among some healthcare professionals that HIPAA and PSQUIA are so focused on patient information privacy, the result is that they, in effect, hinder transparency and inhibit research. Additionally, CLIA mandates that caretakers must provide patients access to their information. Actually HIPAA says something similar, although there have been some extraordinary misunderstandings, such as the now infamous Starbucks barista story, shared by Dr. Cory Franklin in a 2010 *Chicago Tribune* article:

> Recently, at my local Starbucks I asked the barista behind the counter about a medical problem she had that will require surgery. Her answer left me astonished, "Management said I can't talk about my health—it's a HIPAA violation."[73]

The idea that HIPAA regulations apply to everyone, and that patients are not allowed to talk about their own health information, is a common misunderstanding. HIPAA and other privacy regulations actually focus on what healthcare professionals and organizations—not patients—share. Personally identifiable information, clinical data, financial data, and behavioral data is not to be shared or transmitted.[74] While patients can restrict access to their medical data, no one is allowed to prevent patients from accessing their own data. There are debates about what this means. For example, what kind of access is mandated? Is mediated access sufficient? How quickly must access be given when requested? The American Hospital Association has been opposing requests to improve transparency and speed for patient access to their records.[75] At the same time, the US Department of Health and Human Services is levying substantial penalties against hospitals that deny patients access to their medical records.[76] Laws put to protect the privacy of research study participants backfire, and instead deny them access to information to support critical decisions regarding their health.[77]

Within my own online healthcare communities of professionals and patient advocates, there are conversations about these interpretations. Should patients have access to their information? Should the doctors see it first? Should patients share that information, or should health care professionals try to talk them out of it? Who is responsible if a patient does make their information public and then is harmed by having done so? What about identity theft? What about stalking? What about spammers and phishers and snake oil salesmen?

For many years, patients have put their personal medical information online, families sharing with each other to patients sharing with their doctors, and even patients doing their own research studies. Within months after the 2007 release of Google Docs, a group of patients with ALS began using the new tool to collect data on a patient-driven research project to study the use of lithium for the treatment of ALS, with the earliest entry dated December 25, 2007.[78] Since then, Google Health has come and gone, and Microsoft HealthVault is now the leading personal online health information repository, a system known as a patient portal, or personal health records (PHR). PHR are being used right alongside the electronic health records (EHR) for the doctors, and many EHR designed for clinicians are being redesigned to facilitate patient access. Differences between the two are blurring.

Other online services offer private health journaling options, like *CaringBridge*, as well as online support groups and communities, such as *PatientsLikeMe*. Many health communities have public Twitter chats and Facebook groups. Individuals share stories and information with varying levels of candor. People use social media to gather and share information; ask questions; provide answers; dialog with doctors; and save their lives. This has become known as the e-patients movement, which represents "individuals who are equipped, enabled, empowered and engaged in their health and health care decisions."[79] Dave deBronkart is currently the most famous e-patient. After his 2007 diagnosis of Stage IV kidney cancer, the typical survival time was 24 weeks.[80] He recovered and has survived another six years to date. He celebrates annual anniversaries of his "Drop Dead Date" by blowing "razzberries,"[81] and is regularly found speaking at conferences rapping, "Gimme My Damn Data," then being cheered with standing ovations.[82]

People began telling their online stories by blogging, taking photos, recording videos and sending out information 24 hours a day—life-logging, life-streaming, life-casting. Then came smartphones and mobile health, with apps to educate, diagnose, test, and treat. People use phones and other devices—such as the FitBit®—to capture details about their weight, eating, walking, exercise, bicycle paths, sleeping, dreams, heartbeats, insulin levels, salt levels, brain scans, and more. The "quantified self" movement offers opportunities to create big data for everyone. There is enormous potential for learning, distilling discoveries, and creating new approaches to diagnosis and treatment. Dr. Leslie Saxon, a cardiologist from USC and Director of the USC Center for Body Computing, envisioned the *Every Heartbeat* project, which seeks to collect scans of heartbeats of every adult on the planet, to open new avenues of understanding and prevent heart disease through the power of big data.[83] Projects like *23andMe* allow people to share and discuss the personal genomic scans, while *openSNP* allows them to connect their genomic data to their *FitBit* and sleep data.[84,85,86, 87]

For generations, traditional allopathic medicine has focused on the mean, the curve representing the largest group in a statistical bell curves. This is a strength of the discipline, but individuals who are outliers—at one end or the other of the curve—are neglected. Usually, for a rare disease and current methods of studying disease, it is not feasible to gather a significant patient cohort, and design useful studies. I suspect many of us have some aspect of the rare or unique in our family trees. The fields of personalized genomics and personalized medicine are refocusing medicine toward the individual, and away from the mean. Conversely, this massive amount of data will enable new discoveries, because researchers will be able to tap into sufficiently large samples. What is even more revelatory about the quantified self movement is that many people are choosing to make their data publicly available, creating new complications. The anonymous author of *Measured Me* suggests that legal disclaimers should be posted along with data to protect the quantified self-data donor from misuse or abuse by others.[88]

When researchers use online data from patients, the norm is for them to seek consent or permission, or officially partner with the group that has generated the data. This model has proven successful with organizations such as *PatientsLikeMe* and *23andMe*, both of which allow patients to store and access personal health data in combination with community forums for discussion, analysis, sharing, and learning. They offer members opportunities to opt-in to sharing data with research or clinical trials, which have yielded peer-reviewed publications and patents. On social media sites like Twitter and Facebook, public streams—accounts that are unlocked and open to public viewing—are usually considered "fair game." It is not unusual for public streams to unwittingly provide data for research for infodemiology applications, as described by Gunther Eysenbach in his 2009 article.

> Examples for infodemiology applications include: the analysis
> of queries from Internet search engines to predict disease out-

breaks (eg. influenza); monitoring peoples' status updates on microblogs such as Twitter for syndromic surveillance; detecting and quantifying disparities in health information availability; identifying and monitoring of public health relevant publications on the Internet (eg. anti-vaccination sites, but also news articles or expert-curated outbreak reports); automated tools to measure information diffusion and knowledge translation, and tracking the effectiveness of health marketing campaigns.[89]

When the company *23andMe*, a personal genomics service, announced their first patent in May 2012, disgruntled members of their service who had already paid money to participate objected that some members might reap economic benefits from the collective data.[90] Eysenbach acknowledges the issues of privacy and informed consent in infodemiology:

> On the other hand, infodemiology also highlights threats to privacy and raises novel issues around informed consent, due to aggregation and analysis of openly accessible information about people on a large scale."[91]

In their 2012 report, *Privacy and Progress in Whole Genome Sequencing*, the Presidential Commission for the Study of Bioethical Issues masterfully examined the potential benefits and costs of the new technologies while asking how "to reconcile expected societal benefit from advances in whole genome sequencing with privacy risks that fall to the individuals who share their genomic data."[92] This important report identified the primary and tricky dynamics between public benefit and personal risks, and endorsed "the principle of regulatory parsimony, which encourages fostering an achievable balance of intellectual freedom and responsibility." Their recommendations illustrate this dynamic—respect for persons, public beneficence, responsible stewardship, intellectual freedom and responsibility, democratic deliberation, and justice and fairness. The recommendations focused on how to promote collective benefits; provide access to useful data; facilitate scientific progress; and ensure security and consent.

John Wilbanks spearheaded collaborations to develop new consent strategies with his novel and influential project *Consent to Research* (also known by its website address *We Consent Us.*)[93,94] Wilbanks highlights personal agency, control of your own data; structures that encourage patient engagement with research processes and questions; and genomethics, a special branch of bioethics focused on genomics. The result is a simple model, similar in many ways to Creative Commons licensing. But Creative Commons licenses allow individual creators to choose any mix of the criteria attribution, modification, re-sharing, and commercial use. The *Consent to Research* "licenses" are built around the criteria of re-identification, harm, sharing, resharing, and commercial use. Portable Legal Consent (PLC) describes licensing models that allow the creator or contributor of the personal content or data to attach a license to their data describing their desire to be contacted regarding use of the data, thus facilitating discovery, use, adaptation, and re-purposing.

Also noteworthy is IDASH (Integrating Data for Analysis, Anonymization, and Sharing), a government-funded project hosting public and private anonymized data sets, with parallel permissions systems for researchers. Just as *Consent to Research* allows patients to determine how their data will be used, the Data Use Agreements (DUA) from IDASH provide training, and record agreements of understanding—ensuring researchers adhere to limits, like a streamlined and uniform IRB process.[95] The Sage Synapse project, similarly, provides training on human subject data, and related topics.[96]

Zero Sum, Either Or, Yes or No

> *"So in the cages of our consciousness,*
> *The Dove of God is prisoner yet"*
> ~Merton

In this context, it is important to understand why patients and researchers might choose privacy over transparency. Barbara Fister showed us one reason researchers might choose privacy—describing it as a quiet space to develop an idea, or a space where you can hear yourself think. Researchers also seek privacy (and avoid transparency) to protect their ideas—especially if they are working in partnership with a corporate entity—and to safeguard their personal reputations or "brands." Patients might also desire this protectiveness because of fear of stigma, or to secure their physical safety. While the anonymous *Measured Me* is transparent with their data, s/he is less transparent with her or his identity. There have been efforts in several online social spaces—including Facebook, Google+, and Second Life—to require members to use official legal identities as identifiable names in virtual space. These efforts have generated uproars from both supporters and opponents.

I encountered a doctor using Second Life to manage a support group for battered women who shared a revealing story. Some women lived with their abusers, and they could only attend the support group because the abusers belittled Second Life and thought it was an unimportant game, or because they did not know they were using Second Life. Other women were in safe houses, and were able to participate as long as their abusers were unable to locate them. Using a fake name allowed them to participate in the support group; if their true identities were revealed, their lives would be at risk. At the same time, they needed to be able to verify the doctor's identity for their own safety.

A vivid story, which would seem to support transparency, focuses on medical oversight and prevention of medical errors. In a 2012 *Wall Street Journal* article, Dr. Marty Makary tells the story of a charming doctor who is a frighteningly incompetent surgeon, and allowed to practice because of his popularity. He also explores how New York cardiac centers reduced the death rates from surgery by 83% within the first year after being required to report their death rates. One chief surgeon (Doug Rex of Indiana University) videotapes the surgeries done by his staff, assigns a quality score, and tells his staff he will videotape them and score. Quality increases by 30% after they become aware someone is watching. As Makary says, "Nothing makes hospitals shape up more quickly than this kind of public reporting."[97]

We need transparency to support discovery, innovation, and adaptation in our rapidly changing culture. We also need it to create trust for government and large organizations with societal responsibilities. Privacy is essential for safety, including physical and psychological safety, and the security of ideas and evolving ideas.

> In many respects, transparency and privacy occupy opposite ends of a sliding scale. Generally, the more you have of one, the less you have of the other. At the same time, both are distinctly American qualities—privacy to pursue one's interests and happiness without interference from the government or any other institution; transparency to hold government and powerful institutions accountable.[98]

Discussions in the media about these two issues have tended to be polarizing. Possibly the most famous statement illustrating this polarization is from the 1997 Schwartz and Leyden article in *Wired*: "In a nutshell, the key formula for the coming age is this: Open, good. Closed, bad. Tattoo it on your forehead."[99] Authors David Brin and L.S. McGill have debated transparency risks compared to privacy risks, concluding that the risks of transparency are smaller than those for privacy. McGill replied to a comment on her 2012 essay in *Acceler8or*, "The Not-So-Fine Line Between Privacy and Secrecy," with the observation that transparency provides more privacy than we have now.

> There may be sensors, cameras, etc, BUT IF YOU KNOW THEY ARE THERE, AND ARE AWARE IF ANYONE IS USING THEM WITHOUT YOUR PERMISSION, how is it really any different? If the moment someone "peeks" in on you, YOU KNOW WHO IT IS, and whether or not they have your permission to do so? The assumption you ALWAYS make is that your "privacy" will be violatable WITHOUT YOUR KNOWLEDGE. And in a society in which SECRECY IS STILL POSSIBLE, this is possible. IN a society in which SECRECY IS NOT POSSIBLE, your privacy is much more inviolate than it is now.[100]

Brin, in the conclusion to his book *The Transparent Society*, explains his view of the balance, "I am sure of one thing. People of bad intent will be far more free to do harm in a world of secrets, masks, and shrouds than in a realm where the light is growing all around, bit by steady bit."[101] More recently, the famed entrepreneur Peter Thiel expressed the same concept more baldly, "The opposite of transparency is not always privacy.... Sometimes the opposite of transparency is criminality."[102] The arguments for the reverse are equally passionate and persuasive. Solove described the "nothing-to-hide" argument as the most common one used against privacy advocates, and counter arguments boiling down to, "But is it any of your business?"[103] The conversation about privacy and transparency is ill-served by oversimplifications.

> The nothing-to-hide argument speaks to some problems but not to others. It represents a singular and narrow way of conceiving of privacy, and it wins by excluding consideration of the other problems often raised with government security measures. When engaged directly, the nothing-to-hide argument can ensnare, for it forces the debate to focus on its narrow understanding of privacy.[104]

McGill provides a pointed statement to shift this argument slightly off center, "Transparency forces accountability. Secrecy enables an escape from accountability. It really cannot be made any plainer than that."[105] Michael McFarland of the Markkula Center for Applied Ethics at Santa Clara University, argues to protect human dignity, autonomy, control by supporting privacy, and prohibiting abuse and misuse of information.

> Privacy is important for a number of reasons. Some have to do with the consequences of not having privacy. People can be harmed or debilitated if there is no restriction on the public's access to and use of personal information. Other reasons are more fundamental, touching the essence of human personhood. Reverence for the human person as an end in itself and as an autonomous being requires respect for personal privacy. To lose control of one's personal information is in some measure

to lose control of one's life and one's dignity. Therefore, even if privacy is not in itself a fundamental right, it is necessary to protect other fundamental rights.[106]

The assumption of an "either-or" choice is unnecessarily dichotomizing. In the end, these arguments fragment into related concepts and concerns, suggesting this is not a linear argument after all. According to Jane Harman, Chair, Subcommittee on Intelligence, Information Sharing, and Terrorism Risk Assessment:

> Let me be clear, and many have heard me say this over and over and over again, liberty and security are not a zero sum game. We don't get more of one and less of the other. We get more of both or less. In fact, we must get more of both. Security without the liberties that our Constitution protects and Americans treasure is not security.[107]

David Brin agrees. He notes, "transparency is not about eliminating privacy. It is about giving us the power to hold accountable those who would *violate* it."[108]

Introna describes transparency and privacy as concepts that depend on the existence of each other, which cannot be seen without each other, like light and dark, love and sorrow, yin and yang.

> Thus, privacy creates the clearing from which autonomy, trust and accountability can emerge. Ultimately these notions are not the antipodes of privacy. They have privacy as a necessary condition. Privacy is the context of transparency, and transparency is the context of privacy. They are co-constitutive.[109]

PROTE³I

"Open the secret eye of faith."

~Merton

Ethan Bernstein points out a "transparency paradox"—full transparency in the workplace can encourage employees to spend enormous amounts time and energy to create private spaces, or private ways to communicate. Thus, the paradox is that offering employees private spaces may increase their productivity.[110] This contrasts sharply with the previously mentioned study that correlated an increased transparency with an improvement in hospital safety practices. We do not yet understand why transparency would increase productivity and quality of work in one situation, and privacy would do the same in a different situation. This needs further study.

Returning to the earlier discussion of technological gatekeepers and boundary spanning, Allen found that boundary spanning and transparency might only provide a competitive advantage under certain circumstances.

> The concept of technological gatekeeper, therefore, is important only within circumstances. When a subunit (or laboratory) is conducting basic research, gatekeepers are not critical. The organization itself does not impede communication with the outside world. Also the other end of the R&D spectrum, in the subunit concerned with the application of well established technologies to well specified situations, there is little need for gatekeepers. The organization is capable of structuring itself to provide the technical information needed by its members. It is only when the technologies become more complex, in development projects that the need arises for gatekeepers. When the organization (or subunit) is concerned with innovation and is itself contributing to technological advancement, the gatekeeper provides the most effective link between the organization's efforts and those pursued elsewhere.[111]

Perhaps the clearest description of these transparency/privacy or open/closed dichotomies comes from the YouTube video, "John Cleese on Creativity." In this bit, comedian Cleese describes what skills and environments are needed to foster creativity.

[W]e've become fascinated by the fact that we can usefully describe the way in which people function at work in terms of two
modes: open, and closed. So what I can just add now, is that
creativity is NOT possible in the closed mode.... By "closed
mode" I mean the mode that we are in most of the time when
we are at work ... [112]

But, let me make one thing quite clear. We need to be in the open mode
when we're pondering a problem, but, once we come up with a solution,
we must then switch to the closed mode to implement it, because once
we've made a decision, we are efficient *only* if we go through with it deci-
sively, undistracted by doubts about its correctness.[113]

Similarly, at work, when we are planning a new building space, we need
visionary thought in the planning stages to anticipate future needs. But
at some point we need to stop, decide on a blueprint, and build it. The
pendulum swings, back and forth, open or closed, creative or productive,
with both needed at different times in the lifespan of the same project. The
"opposites" are not necessarily "opposites," but shifting points within the
life cycles of object, innovations, individuals, and art.

Vice-versa. Improvisation. The 'opposites' are thought of not
as different things, but as opposites. So, notations permitting
various realizations are inside square, rectangular, or circular
areas. Where there is no choice, everything follows conventions.[114]

Here is a model that I hope will provide a framework to integrate and
explore nuances of these non-linear issues. It was developed from close
observation and discussion of these issues in social media over several
years. It is based on observation rather than data and I welcome further
discussion and testing. PROTE³I stands for the components of this model: Privacy, Reciprocity, Options, Transparency, Equilibrium, Exploration,
Enterprise, and Individual. The model is constructed in three layers—Dynamic, Purpose, and Role.

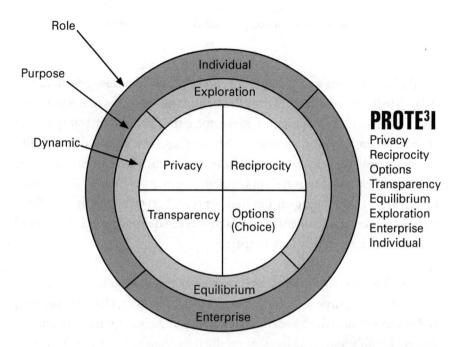

Figure. 9.1. Privacy, Reciprocity, Options, Transparency, Equilibrium, Exploration, Enterprise, and Individual Model

The "Dynamic" layer refers to most of what has been discussed so far. In the PROTE³I model, both privacy and transparency are modified by reciprocity, and options. Briefly, if one is in private mode, there is an implied expectation that others will respect that privacy, and will not violate it or intrude into it. Likewise, if one is in transparent mode, there is a similar expectation. Patients who have chosen to be transparent with health information or personal data expect that researchers using that data or information will be equally transparent and forthcoming. When people provide information about their behavior to Google or Facebook, or allow their statuses, photos, and searches to be captured, the concern is often less about the actual information provided, but about their desire for Google and Facebook to be equally transparent about how our data is being used. People often do not mind their data being used, as long as they can also see all their data; see how it is being used; and have equal information about those using it. In each of these modes—private or transparent—when others do not reciprocate there is a sense of inequality and unfairness.

Similarly, in private and transparent modes, there is a desire to have options—to have some control over the boundaries and uses of the information. There is more willingness to accept either privacy or transparency as valid when limits on each are made explicit, and clearly defined. The choices people usually emphasize have been articulated in the licensing structures discussed above, from *Creative Commons* to *Consent To Research* to *iDASH*, each defining an implied contract between creator and those who use the created content. This is a process of defining expectations and norms, and these ideally lead to trust.

The middle layer is "Purpose," and represents the shifting between modes. Exploring is the purpose that requires openness, creativity, play, transparency, and collaboration, which generates new ideas, strategies, approaches, and solutions. Equilibrium is the time for production-focused behaviors. The outer layer is "Roles." We may strongly support transparency in support of the work we do for our job and still insist upon privacy in our personal lives, or the reverse. We may switch from being an advocate for one or the other depending upon the role we are play and whose interests are being represented.

Conclusion: The Burning Barn

> *"The weak walls Of the world fall."*
> ~Merton

Ultimately, this is all about building trust through openness and security, accountability, and managed risks. Debates about transparency and privacy are volatile, and transparency and risk have the potential to destroy what they are trying to save, and inhibit what (or who) they are trying to empower. McGill is correct to point out that conversations about transparency and privacy should not be equated with discussions about accountability and secrecy. The conversations should, perhaps, be focused more on who has control; who makes the choices; how choices are enforced; and how do we see accountability. In his essay titled "What Is and What Should Be the Role of Scientific Culture in Modern Society," physicist Richard Feynman wrote:

> I believe that one of the greatest dangers to modern society is the possible resurgence and expansion of the ideas of thought control; such ideas as Hitler had, or Stalin in his time, of the Catholic religion in the Middle Ages, or the Chinese today. I think that one of the greatest dangers is that this shall increase until it encompasses all of the world." [115]

In his book *The Transparent Society*, David Brin details what happens when governments are neither transparent nor accountable, with names and years spelled out, over and over again. Barbara Fister said she had concerns were about the lack of reciprocity in the data our online systems gather from us; in short, she thought it was unfair for us not know everything about our data, because we generate and create that data.

> What happens if this mania for gathering private information passes and the business model proves unsustainable? What if it's all a bubble? We may have to find new ways to search and share. And maybe next time we'll avoid building it as a front for a massive surveillance system. [116]

David often argues in favor of sousveillance (monitoring from below) in contrast to surveillance (monitoring from above). The way we perceive the constant battling about Facebook's ever changing privacy features would radically change if we could assume that the information is for us, instead of for Facebook. It would also read differently if people had the power to determine who has access to their data, and what can be done with it. I do not just mean "opt-in or opt-out power," but also options to manage access and use of your data. Echoes of this discussion are in the earliest writings on professional ethics in librarianship.

> Today indications in many parts of the world point to growing intolerance, suppression of free speech, and censorship affecting the rights of minorities and individuals. [117]

The epigraphs in this chapter are excerpted from a Thomas Merton poem about the nighttime prayer life at the Abbey of Gethsemani. Another poem in the same book describes another night, and the beauty of the burning barn at the Abbey of Gethsemani, where he lived. We know what barns are—large farm buildings where we keep animals, vehicles, and stored food. They also serve as workspaces for large projects separate from the living space. In modern suburban life, they would be a merger between a garage and an oversized pantry. As an intellectual metaphor, the barn could represent structures that contain and preserve the products and processes of scholarship and science: the libraries, museums, publishing houses, R&D labs, universities, research centers, and perhaps, even the internet.

At Gethsemani, what did the monks do when the barn burned? They ran to rescue the livestock and animals, to remove as much as possible of what they had saved earlier. They probably formed a bucket brigade to douse the fire, then stood back to watch it burn, beautifully. Afterward, they built a new barn, not quite like the one they had before. We are in the process now of building new barns.

ACKNOWLEDGEMENTS

All epigraphs are selected from Thomas Merton's poem, "After the Night Office—Gethsemani Abbey."

Thanks to David Brin for reviewing an early version of the PROTE³I model.

NOTES

1. B. Fister, "The Value of Doing Research—and Sharing It," *Inside Higher Ed: Library Babel Fish*, December 19 2011, accessed May 09 2012, http://www.insidehighered.com/blogs/value-doing-research-and-sharing-it.
2. B. Fister, "I'm Not Buying It: The Importance of Privacy for Research," *Inside Higher Ed:Library Babel Fish*, February 1 2012, accessed May 09 2012, http://www.insidehighered.com/blogs/i'm-not-buying-it-importance-privacy-research.
3. B. Fister, "The Value of Doing Research—and Sharing It," *Inside Higher Ed: Library Babel Fish*, December 19 2011, accessed May 09 2012, http://www.insidehighered.com/blogs/value-doing-research-and-sharing-it.
4. Ibid.
5. B. Fister, "I'm Not Buying It: The Importance of Privacy for Research," *Inside Higher Ed:Library Babel Fish*, February 1 2012, accessed May 09 2012, http://www.insidehighered.com/blogs/i'm-not-buying-it-importance-privacy-research.

6. E. Pariser, *The Filter Bubble: What the Internet Is Hiding From You* (NY: Penguin, 2011).

7. B. Fister, "I'm Not Buying It: The Importance of Privacy for Research," *Inside Higher Ed:Library Babel Fish*, February 1 2012, accessed May 09 2012, http://www.insidehighered.com/blogs/i'm-not-buying-it-importance-privacy-research.

8. E. A. Zerhouni, "Translational and Clinical Science—Time for a New Vision," *N Engl J Med*, no. 353 (2005):1621-1623, accessed November 9, 2012, http://www.nejm.org/toc/nejm/353/15/.

9. Ibid.

10. US National Library of Medicine. Citations Added to MEDLINE by Fiscal Year. http://www.nlm.nih.gov/bsd/stats/cit_added.html Updated March 22, 2013. Retrieved May 13, 2013.

11. Ibid.

12. T. J Allen, *Managing the Flow of Technology* (MA: MIT Press, 1997).

13. Ibid, 1

14. Ibid, 3

15. Ibid, 13.

16. P. R. Spence and M.C. Reddy, "The 'active' Gatekeeper in Collaborative Information Seeking Activities," *Proceedings of the 2007 International ACM Conference on Supporting Group Work* (2007):277-280.

17. P. R. Spence with M.C. Reddy, "Beyond Expertise Seeking: A Field Study of Informal Knowledge Practices of Healthcare IT Teams," *Computer Supported Cooperative Work*, no. 21(2-3) (2012):283-315.

18. D. Crane, *Invisible Colleges; Diffusion of Knowledge In Scientific Communities* (Chicago: University of Chicago Press, 1972).

19. C. S. Wagner, *The New Invisible College : Science for Development* (Washington, DC: Brookings Institution Press, 2008).

20. M. Kochen and Karl W. Deutsch, "Decentralization: Toward Rational Theory," *Science Center Berlin* 21, (1980).

21. L. Swanson, "Fish Oil, Raynaud's Syndrome, and undiscovered public knowledge," *Perspect Biology Med* 30, no. 1 (1986):7-18.

22. R.A. DiGiacomo and J.M. Kremer and D.M. Shah "Fish-oil dietary supplementation in patients with Raynuad's Phenomenon: a double-blinded, controlled, prospective study," *Am J Med* 86, no. 2 (1989):158-64.

23. L. Swanson, "Migraine and Magnesium: Eleven Neglected Connections," *Perspect Biol Med* 31, no. 4 (1988):526-57.

24. L. Swanson, "A Second Example of Mutually Isolated medical Literatures Related by implicit, Unnoticed Connections," *J Am Soc Inf Sci* 40, no. 6 (1989):432-5.

25. N.M. Ramadan et al, "Low Brain Magnesium in Migraine," *Headache* 29, no. 7 (1989):416-9.

26. N.M. Ramadan et al, "Low Brain Magnesium in Migraine," *Headache* 29, no. 9 (1989):590-3.

27. K Taubert "Magnesium bei Migrane. Ergebnisse einer multizentrischen Pilotstudie [Magnesium in Migraine. Results of a Multicenter Pilot Study]," *Fortschr Med* 20, no. 24 (1994):328-30.

28. K Taubert "Magnesium bei Migrane. Ergebnisse einer multizentrischen Pilotstudie [Magnesium in Migraine. Results of a Multicenter Pilot Study]," *Fortschr Med* 20, no. 24 (1994):328-30.

29. A Mauskop et al, "Intravenous Magnesium Sulphate Relieves Migraine Attacks In Patients

with Low Serum Ionized Magnesium Levels: A Pilot Study," *Clinical Science (Lond)* 89, no. 6 (1995):633-6.

30. H.C. Diener et al, "A Practical Guide to the Management and Prevention of Migraine," *Drugs* 56, no. 5 (1998):811-24.

31. S. Holland et al, "Quality Standards Subcommittee of the American Academy of Neurology and the American Headache Society. Evidence-based guideline update: NSAIDS and other complementary treatments for episodic migraine prevention in adults: report of the Quality Standards Subcommittee of the American Academy of Neurology and the American Headache Association," *Neurology* 78, no. 17 (2012):1346-53.

32. T. Pringsheim et al, "Canadian Headache Society Prophylactic Guidelines Development Group. Canadian Headache Society guideline for migraine prophylaxis," *Canadian Journal of Neurological Sciences* 39, no. 2 (2012):S1-59.

33. TJ Allen, Roles in Technical Communication Networks. *MIT*, Alfred P. Sloan School of Management, Working Paper, December 1969, #434-69. Accessed April 10, 2012. http://18.7.29.232/bitstream/handle/1721.1/48979/rolesintechnical00alle.pdf?sequence=1.

34. ZS, Morris, S Wooding, J Grant. "The answer is 17 years, What is the question: understanding time lags in translational research." *J R Soc Med* 104 (2011): 510–520. DOI 10.1258/jrsm.2011.110180.

35. Ibid.

36. Ibid.

37. D. Brin, *The Transparent Society* (MA: Perseus Books, 1998).

38. D. Brin, "The Value—and Empowerment—of Common Citizens in and Age of Danger," *The Futurist*, 2001, November 15, 2012, http://www.futurist.com/articles-archive/society-and-culture/value-and-empowerment/

39. Ibid.

40. NIH Public Access Mandate: http://publicaccess.nih.gov, retrieved March 18, 2013.

41. B. Merz, "Nobelists take genetics from bench to bedside," *JAMA* 254, no. 22 (1944, 1967):48-49.

42. NIH Clinical Center "NIH Beside-to-Bench Program: New! Program Changes Name," *NIH Clinical Center*, 2012, http://clinicalcenter.nih.gov/ccc/btb/.

43. Cancer.gov "Research to Reality,"*Cancer.gov*, 2011, accessed September 29, 2012, https://researchtoreality.cancer.gov/.

44. JI, Gallin. NIHClinicalCenter (Poster) (2012, June 12) The Bedside-to-Bench Award Program [Video] Retrieved from http://www.youtube.com/watch?v=zl2TH7K-piQ

45. J. Kotz "Bringing patient data into the open," *Science-Business eXchange* 5, no. 25 (2012): accessed November 21, 2012. http://www.nature.com/scibx/journal/v5/n25/full/scibx.2012.644.html

46. "Training for Consumer Referees." *Cochrane Consumer Network*, accessed November 2, 2012, http://consumers.cochrane.org/refereetraining/

47. "Consumer Participation."*Cochrane Consumer Network*, November 2, 2012, http://consumers.cochrane.org/consumer-participation

48. "Christmas Bird Count" *National Audubon Society*, accessed November 13, 2012, http://birds.audubon.org/christmas-bird-count

49. American Birds, 2010-2011, the annual summary of the Christmas Bird Count, volume 65."*National Audubon Society*, accessed November 13, 2012, http://birds.audubon.org/american-birds-2010-2011-summary-111th-christmas-bird-count

50. "Audubon to Expand Famous Christmas Bird Count 113th Annual Holiday Count to 'Drop Fees, Add Languages, Go Digital.'" *National Audubon Society*, October 23, 2012. Ac-

cessed November 13, 2012, http://www.audubon.org/newsroom/press-releases/2012/audubon-expand-famous-christmas-bird-count

51. C.J Lintott et al, "'Hanny's Voorwerp', a quasar light echo?," *Monthly Notices of the Royal Astronomical Society* 399, no. 1 (2009):129-140.

52. P. Gay, "Citizen Science" *MICA Seminar Series*, August 22, 2009, accessed November 14, 2012, http://www.mica-vw.org/wiki/index.php/Citizen_Science

53. "MICA Seminar Descriptions and Info," *Asterisk: Astronomy Picture of the Day's footnote*, accessed May 14, 2012, http://asterisk.apod.com/ampersand/?page_id=123

54. E. Kintisch, "How to Grow Your Own Army of Citizen Scientists" *Science Insider*, February 24 2011, accessed November 14, 2012, http://news.sciencemag.org/scienceinsider/2011/02/how-to-grow-your-own-army-of.html

55. V. Arkel, "H. 04 | Voorwerp: The Story Behind." *Hanny's Voorwerp*, November 18, 2008, Accessed November 14, 2012. http://www.hannysvoorwerp.com/?page_id=8

56. C.J Lintott et al, "'Hanny's Voorwerp', a quasar light echo?," *Monthly Notices of the Royal Astronomical Society* 399, no. 1 (2009):129-140.

57. L. Horn "Gamers Unlock Protein Mystery That Baffled AIDS Researchers For Years," *PC Magazine*, accessed September 19, 2012. http://www.pcmag.com/article2/0,2817,2393200,00.asp

58. MJ. Coren "Foldit Gamers Solve Riddle of HIV Enzyme within 3 Weeks," *Scientific American*, September 20, 2011, accessed September 19, 2012. http://www.scientificamerican.com/article.cfm?id=foldit-gamers-solve-riddle

59. F. Khatib et al, "Crystal structure of a monomeric retroviral protease solved by protein folding game players," *Nature Structural & Molecular Biology*, September 18, 2011, accessed November 15, 2012, http://homes.cs.washington.edu/~zoran/NSMBfoldit-2011.pdf

60. P. Plait "Voorwerp! Bad Astronomy," *Discover Magazine*, September 20, 2011, accessed November 13 2012, http://blogs.discovermagazine.com/badastronomy/2011/01/11/voorwerp/

61. ATLAS Collaboration "Combined search for the Standard Model Higgs boson using up to 4.9 fb^{-1} of pp collision data at $\sqrt{s}$ = 7 TeV with the ATLAS detector at the LHC," *Psychics Letter B* 710, (2012):49-66.

62. Jaime A Teixeira da Silva, "The ethics of collaborative authorship," *EMBRO reports* 12, no. 9 (2011):889-893, accessed November 15, 2012, http://www.nejm.org/toc/nejm/353/15/.

63. MMV(Medicines for Malaria Venture) "Open Access Malaria Box," accessed November 15 2012, http://www.mmv.org/malariabox

64. A.E. Williamson et al, "Open Source Drug Discovery—Malaria," accessed November 15 2012, http://openwetware.org/wiki/Open_Source_Drug_Discovery_-_Malaria

65. A.E. Williamson et al, "Open Source Drug Discovery—Malaria," accessed November 15 2012, http://openwetware.org/wiki/Open_Source_Drug_Discovery_-_Malaria

66. C. Årdal and J-A Røttingen, "Open Source Drug Discovery in Practice: A Case Study," *PLoS Negl Trop Dis* 6, no. 9 (1827): accessed November 13, 2012, http://www.plosntds.org/article/info%3Adoi%2F10.1371%2Fjournal.pntd.0001827

67. AG Lisi "An Exceptionally Simple Theory of Everything." *Arxiv.org*, November 6, 2007, accessed November 15, 2012, http://arxiv.org/abs/0711.0770

68. R. Highfield "Surfer dude stuns physicists with theory of everything," *The Telegraph*, November 6, 2007 6:02 PM GMT, accessed November 15, 2012 , http://www.telegraph.co.uk/science/large-hadron-collider/3314456/Surfer-dude-stuns-physicists-with-theory-of-everything.html

69. Health Information Privacy. http://www.hhs.gov/ocr/privacy/, Retrieved March 18, 2013.

70. Patient Safety and Quality Improvement Act of 2005 Statute and Rule, http://www.hhs.gov/ocr/privacy/psa/regulation/index.html , Retrieved March 18, 2013.

71. Patient Protection and Affordable Care Act, http://www.gpo.gov/fdsys/pkg/PLAW-111publ148/pdf/PLAW-111publ148.pdf, Retrieved March 18, 2013.

72. T. Huelskamp "Political Realities: Privacy Concerns In The Affordable Care Act.," September 27, 2011, accessed November 18, 2012, http://huelskamp.house.gov/index.php?option=com_content&view=article&id=3663

73. C. Franklin, *Interview in Chicago Tribune*, 2010.

74. C. Ascenzo, "4 big data threats health org's are socially obligated to safeguard against," *Government Health IT*, September 20, 2012, accessed November 13, 2012, http://www.govhealthit.com/blog/4-big-data-threats-health-org%E2%80%99s-are-socially-obligated-safeguard-against

75. D. McGraw "Hospital Association Fights Digital Data Access for Patients," *Center for Democracy and Technology*, May 2, 2012, accessed November 20, 2012, https://www.cdt.org/blogs/deven-mcgraw/0205hospital-association-fights-digital-data-access-patients

76. US. Department of Health and Human Services, "HHS imposes a $4.3 million civil money penalty for violations of the HIPAA Privacy Rule," *DHHS*, February 22, 2011, accessed November 20, 2012, http://www.hhs.gov/news/press/2011pres/02/20110222a.html

77. J. Lauerman, "College or funeral is mother's wish denied on DNA results," *Bloomberg Businessweek*, May 14, 2012, accessed November 20, 2012, http://www.businessweek.com/news/2012-05-14/will-my-baby-die-dna-revelation-comes-too-late

78. Macedo H, Felzer K., "Lithium Worldwide Survey." 2008, accessed May 14, 2013, https://spreadsheets.google.com/pub?key=pq7l2D-lVjOcsItCl6frJMA

79. e-patients.net. http://e-patients.net/about-e-patientsnet, Retrieved March 18, 2013.

80. D. Debronkart, "My Cancer Story—Short Version," *The New Life of e-Patient Dave*, June 19 2008, accessed November 09, 2012, http://patientdave.blogspot.com/2008/06/my-cancer-story-short-version.html

81. D. Debronkart, "It's my Drop Dead Date plus three years. Thppppt!," *The New Life of e-Patient Dave*, June 26 2010, accessed November 18, 2012, http://patientdave.blogspot.com/2010/06/its-drop-dead-date-plus-three-years.html

82. D. deBronkart (Creator). WellApps (Poster) (2011, July 27) Gimme My Damn Data by e-patient Dave deBronkart . [Video] Retrieved from http://www.youtube.com/watch?v=0b4li7N_7Ck

83. Gaglani S., "Gaglani's Gadgets: Dr. Leslie Saxon and the Center for Body Computing—A New Era in Cardio Technology and Monitoring?" American College of Cardiology Cardiosource. August 9, 2012. http://www.cardiosource.org/News-Media/Publications/CardioSource-World-News/Gaglanis-Gadgets.aspx, Retrieved May 13, 2013.

84. openSNP, http://opensnp.org/, Retrieved March 18, 2013.

85. everyheartbeat.org, http://www.everyheartbeat.org/, Retrieved March 18, 2013.

86. Fitbit, http://www.fitbit.com/, Retrieved March 18, 2013.

87. 23andMe, https://www.23andme.com/, Retrieved March 18, 2013.

88. "Should Quantified Self Researchers Protect Themselves with Disclaimers?," *Measured Me*, October 12, 2012, accessed November 18, 2012, http://www.measuredme.com/2012/10/should-quantified-self-researchers-protect-themselves-with-disclaimers.html

89. G. Eysenbach, "Infodemiology and Infoveillance: Framework for an Emerging Set of Public Health Informatics: Methods to Analyze Search, Communication and Publication

Behavior on the Internet.," *J Med Internet* 11, no. 1 (2009):e11, accessed May 09, 2012, http://www.jmir.org/2009/1/e11

90. E.C. Hayden, " Informed consent: A broken contract," *Nature 486,* (2009):312-314.

91. G. Eysenbach, "Infodemiology and Infoveillance: Framework for an Emerging Set of Public Health Informatics: Methods to Analyze Search, Communication and Publication Behavior on the Internet.," *J Med Internet* 11, no. 1 (2009):e11, accessed May 09, 2012, http://www.jmir.org/2009/1/e11

92. A. Gutmann et al, "Privacy and Progress in Whole Genome Sequencing.," *Washington, DC: Presidential Commission for the Study of Bioethical Issues,* (2009): accessed November 20, 2012, http://www.bioethics.gov/cms/sites/default/files/PrivacyProgress508.pdf

93. J. Wilbanks with consent to research, September 18, 2011, accessed November 20, 2012, http://www.slideshare.net/wilbanks/consent-to-research

94. Wilbanks J with consent to Research, *iDASH webinar,* Mar 16, 2012, accessed November 20, 2012, http://www.slideshare.net/wilbanks/consent-to-research-idash-webinar

95. iDASH, http://idash.ucsd.edu/, Retrieved on March 18, 2013.

96. Sage Bionetworks Synapse, http://sagebase.org/research/Synapse1.php, Retrieved March 18, 2013.

97. M. Makary, "How to Stop Hospitals From Killing Us.," *Wall Street Journal* (2012): accessed November 20, 2012, http://online.wsj.com/article/SB10000872396390444620104578008263334441352.html

98. R. Dryer, J. Corper, V, Craigle, A. Boren, M. Carpenter, I, Ghabash, T, Gould, L. Gren, N, Harris, T, Krause, C, Oman, A, Tripp, T, Tu. Transparency and privacy, clashing paradigms in a Web 2.0 world. (A University of Utah Honors Think Tank 2012)

99. O Schwartz and P. Leyden "The Long Boom: A History of the Future, 1980-2020,"*Wired July,* 1997, accessed November 21, 2012, http://www.wired.com/wired/archive/5.07/longboom_pr.html

100. L.S. McGill "The Not-so-fine line between privacy and secrecy," *Institute for Ethics and Emerging Technologies,* June 30, 2012, accessed November 14, 2012, http://ieet.org/index.php/IEET/more/6026

101. D. Brin, *The Transparent Society* (MA: Perseus Books, 1998).

102. H. MacKenzie. "Peter Thiel: Sometimes the opposite of transparency is criminality." *Pando-Daily,* April 19, 2012, accessed November 21, 2012 http://pandodaily.com/2012/04/19/peter-thiel-sometimes-the-opposite-of-transparency-is-criminality/

103. D.J. Solove. "Why privacy matters even if you have 'nothing to hide,'" *Chronicle Review,* May 15, 2011, accessed November 21, 2012, http://chronicle.com/article/Why-Privacy-Matters-Even-if/127461/

104. Ibid.

105. L.S. McGill "The Not-so-fine line between privacy and secrecy," *Institute for Ethics and Emerging Technologies,* June 30, 2012, accessed November 14, 2012, http://ieet.org/index.php/IEET/more/6026

106. M. McFarland "Why we care about privacy," *Santa Clara University, Markulla Center for Applied Ethics.,* accessed November 21, 2012, http://www.scu.edu/ethics/practicing/focusareas/technology/internet/privacy/why-care-about-privacy.html

107. US. House of Representatives. Committee on Homeland Security. "Internet terror recruitment & tradecraft: How can we address an evolving tool while protecting free speech? Hearing before the Subcommittee on Intelligence, Information Sharing, and Terrorism Risk Assessment of the Committee on Homeland Security, House of Representatives," *One Hundred Eleventh Congress, Second Session, May 26, 2010,* no. 111-67 accessed No-

vember 20, 2012, http://www.gpo.gov/fdsys/pkg/CHRG-111hhrg63091/html/CHRG-111hhrg63091.htm.

108.   D. Brin, *The Transparent Society* (MA: Perseus Books, 1998).

109.   L.D. Introna, "Privacy and the computer: why we need privacy in the information society," *Metaphilosophy* 28, no. 3 (1997):259-275.

110.   E. Bernstein, "The Transparency Paradox: A Role for Privacy in Organizational Learning and Operational Control," *Admin Sci Q* 57, no. 2 (2012):181-216.

111.   T.J. Allen et al, "Technology Transfer as a Function of Position in the Spectrum from Research through Development to Technical Services," *The Academy of Management Journal* 22, no. 4 (1979):694-708, accessed September 29, 2012, http://www.jstor.org/stable/255809.

112.   John J. Cleese (Creator). wuvwebs(Poster) (2012, March 23) Cleese J. John Cleese on Creativity [Video] from http://www.youtube.com/watch?v=VShmtsLhkQg.

113.   Ibid.

114.   J. Cage, Notations, West Glover, VT, 1969, 34.

115.   R. Feynman, The Pleasure of Finding Things Out. Cambridge, MA: Perseus Books, 1999.

116.   B. Fister, "I'm Not Buying It: The Importance of Privacy for Research," *Inside Higher Ed:Library Babel Fish*, February 1 2012, accessed May 09 2012, http://www.insidehighered.com/blogs/i'm-not-buying-it-importance-privacy-research.

117.   Louise S. Robbins, The Library's Bill of Rights Censorship and the American Library: *The American Library Associations' Response to Threats to Intellectual Freedom 1939-1969* (Westport, CT: Greenwood Press, 1996).

BIBLIOGRAPHY

Allen TJ. *Managing the Flow of Technology*. Cambridge, MA: MIT Press, 1977.

Allen TJ, Tushman ML, Lee DMS. "Technology Transfer as a Function of Position in the Spectrum from Research through Development to Technical Services." *The Academy of Management Journal*, Vol. 22, No. 4 (Dec., 1979), pp. 694-708. Accessed September 29, 2012.http://www.jstor.org/stable/255809.

Allen TJ. *Roles in Technical Communication Networks*. MIT, Alfred P. Sloan School of Management, Working Paper, December 1969, #434-69. Accessed April 10, 2012.http://18.7.29.232/bitstream/handle/1721.1/48979/rolesintechnical00alle.pdf?sequence=1.

Årdal C, Røttingen J-A. "Open Source Drug Discovery in Practice: A Case Study." *PLoS Negl Trop Dis 2012 6(9): e1827. doi:10.1371/journal.pntd.0001827*. Accessed November 13, 2012. http://www.plosntds.org/article/info%3Adoi%2F10.1371%2Fjournal.pntd.0001827.

Ascenzo C. "4 big data threats health org's are socially obligated to safeguard against." *Government Health IT, September 20, 2012*. Accessed November 18, 2012. http://www.govhealthit.com/blog/4-big-data-threats-health-org%E2%80%99s-are-socially-obligated-safeguard-against.

Asterisk. "MICA Seminar Descriptions and Info." Asterisk: Astronomy Picture of the Day's footnote (blog). Accessed November 14, 2012. http://asterisk.apod.com/ampersand/?page_id=123.

ATLAS Collaboration. "Combined search for the Standard Model Higgs boson using up to 4.9 fb^{-1} of pp collision data at $\sqrt{s}$ = 7 TeV with the ATLAS detector at the LHC." *Physics Letters B* (2012) 710:49–66.

"The Bedside-to-Bench Award Program." June 12, 2012. YouTube video, 1:35, from a personal interview. Posted by "NIHClinicalCenter." Accessed September 29, 2012. http://www.youtube.com/watch?v=zl2TH7K-piQ.

Bernstein E. *The Transparency Paradox: A Role for Privacy in Organizational Learning and Opera-*

tional Control. Admin Sci Q 2012 57(2):181-216.

Boylan P. "Do vs Jutsu. Again." The Budo Bum. November 15, 2012. Accessed November 20, 2012. http://budobum.blogspot.com/2012/11/do-vs-jutsu-again.html.

Brin D. *The Transparent Society.* Reading, MA: Perseus Books, ©1998.

Brin D. "The Value—and Empowerment—of Common Citizens in an Age of Danger." The Futurist. 2001. Accessed November 15, 2012. http://www.futurist.com/articles-archive/society-and-culture/value-and-empowerment/.

Cancer.gov. "Research to Reality." 2011. Accessed September 29, 2012. https://researchtoreality.cancer.gov/.

"John Cleese on Creativity. Webster University Vienna MSV2." Mar 23, 2012. YouTube video, 36:10, from a talk given at Webster University. Posted by "wuvwebs." Accessed November 20, 2012. http://www.youtube.com/watch?v=VShmtsLhkQg.

Cochrane Collaboration(a). "Cochrane Consumer Network: Training for Consumer Referees." Accessed November 2, 2012. http://consumers.cochrane.org/refereetraining/.

Cochrane Collaboration(b). "Cochrane Consumer Network: Consumer participation." Accessed November 2, 2012. http://consumers.cochrane.org/consumer-participation .

Coren MJ. "Foldit Gamers Solve Riddle of HIV Enzyme within 3 Weeks." Scientific American, September 20, 2011. Accessed November 15, 2012. http://www.scientificamerican.com/article.cfm?id=foldit-gamers-solve-riddle.

Crane D. *Invisible colleges; diffusion of knowledge in scientific communities.* Chicago, IL: University of Chicago Press, 1972.

da Silva JAT. "The ethics of collaborative authorship." *EMBO Rep.* 2011 September; 12(9): 889–893. doi: 10.1038/embor.2011.161. Accessed November 15, 2012. http://www.ncbi.nlm.nih.gov/pmc/articles/PMC3166465/

deBronkart D. "It's my Drop Dead Date plus three years. Thppppt!" The New Life of e-Patient Dave June 26, 2010. Accessed November 18, 2012.http://patientdave.blogspot.com/2010/06/its-drop-dead-date-plus-three-years.html.

deBronkart D." My cancer story—short version." The New Life of e-Patient Dave, June 18, 2008. Accessed November 18, 2012. http://patientdave.blogspot.com/2008/06/my-cancer-story-short-version.html.

Diener HC, H Kaube and V Limmroth. "A practical guide to the management and prevention of migraine." *Drugs.* 56 no. 5 November(1998):811-24.

DiGiacomo RA, JM Kremer and DM Shah. "Fish-oil dietary supplementation in patients with Raynaud's phenomenon: a double-blind, controlled, prospective study." *Am J Med.* 86 no. 2 February(1989):158-64.

Eysenbach G. "Infodemiology and Infoveillance: Framework for an Emerging Set of Public Health Informatics: Methods to Analyze Search, Communication and Publication Behavior on the Internet." *J Med Internet Res* 11 no. 1 (2009):e11. Accessed May 9, 2012. http://www.jmir.org/2009/1/e11.

Fister B. "The Value of Doing Research—and Sharing It." Inside Higher Ed: Library Babel Fish December 19, 2011; 10:24pm. Accessed May 9, 2012. http://www.insidehighered.com/blogs/value-doing-research-and-sharing-it.

Fister B. "I'm Not Buying It: The Importance of Privacy for Research." Inside Higher Ed: Library Babel Fish. February 1, 2012; 8:40pm. Accessed May 9, 2012. http://www.insidehighered.com/blogs/i'm-not-buying-it-importance-privacy-research.

Galaxy Zoo. "The Story So Far." Accessed November 14, 2012. http://www.galaxyzoo.org/#/story.

Gay P. *Citizen Science.* MICA Seminar Series. August 22, 2009 at 10:00 AM PDT. Accessed November 14, 2012. http://www.mica-vw.org/wiki/index.php/Citizen_Science.

"Gimme My Damn Data by e-patient Dave deBronkart." Jul 27, 2011. YouTube video, 0:45, from a performance of TED Talks. Posted by "WellApps." Accessed November 18, 2012. http://www.youtube.com/watch?v=0b4li7N_7Ck.

Harpham GG. "Why We Need the 16,772nd Book on Shakespeare." *Qui Parle* 20 no. 1 (2011):109-116.

Hayden EC. "Informed consent: A broken contract." *Nature* (2012) 486:312-314.

Health Economics Research Group, Office of Health Economics, RAND Europe. *Medical Research: What's it Worth? Estimating the Economic Benefits from Medical Research in the UK.* London: UK Evaluation Forum, 2008. Accessed November 14, 2012. http://www.wellcome.ac.uk/stellent/groups/corporatesite/@sitestudioobjects/documents/web_document/wtx052110.pdf.

Highfield R. "Surfer dude stuns physicists with theory of everything." *The Telegraph*, November 14, 2007 6:02PM GMT. Accessed November 15, 2012. http://www.telegraph.co.uk/science/large-hadron-collider/3314456/Surfer-dude-stuns-physicists-with-theory-of-everything.html.

Holland S, SD Silberstein, F Freitag, DW Dodick, C Argoff, E Ashman; Quality Standards Subcommittee of the American Academy of Neurology and the American Headache Society. "Evidence-based guideline update: NSAIDs and other complementary treatments for episodic migraine prevention in adults: report of the Quality Standards Subcommittee of the American Academy of Neurology and the American Headache Society." *Neurology.* 78 no. 17 (April 24, 2012):1346-53.

Horn L. "Gamers Unlock Protein Mystery That Baffled AIDS Researchers For Years." PC Magazine, September 19, 2011 10:42am EST. Accessed November 15, 2012 http://www.pcmag.com/article2/0,2817,2393200,00.asp.

Huelskamp T. "Political Realities: Privacy Concerns In The Affordable Care Act." Tuesday, September 27, 2011. Accessed November 18, 2012. http://huelskamp.house.gov/index.php?option=com_content&view=article&id=3663.

Introna LD. "Privacy and the computer: Why we need privacy in the information society." *Metaphilosophy* 28 no. 3 (1997):259-275.

Kintisch E. "How to grow your own army of citizen scientists." Science Insider. February 24, 2011, 11:45 AM. Accessed November 14, 2012. http://news.sciencemag.org/scienceinsider/2011/02/how-to-grow-your-own-army-of.html.

Khatib F, F DiMaio, FoldIt Contenders Group, FoldIt Void Crushers Group, S Cooper, M Kazmierczyk, M Gilski, S Krzywda, H Zabranska, I Pichova, J Thompson, Z Popovic, M Jazkolski, D Baker. *Crystal structure of a monomeric retroviral protease solved by protein folding game players.* Nature Structural & Molecular Biology published online September 18, 2011; doi:10.1038/nsmb.2119. Accessed November 15, 2012. http://homes.cs.washington.edu/~zoran/NSMBfoldit-2011.pdf.

Kochen M and KW Deutsch. *Decentralization: Toward a Rational Theory. (Wissenschaftszentrum Berlin. Publication of the Science Center Berlin; v. 21.)* Cambridge, MA: Oelgeschlager, Gunn & Hain, ©1980.

Kotz J. "Bringing patient data into the open." *SciBX* 5 no. 25 (2012); doi:10.1038/scibx.2012.644. Accessed November 21, 2012. http://www.nature.com/scibx/journal/v5/n25/full/scibx.2012.644.html.

Lauerman J. "College or funeral is mother's wish denied on DNA results." *Bloomberg Businessweek* May 14, 2012. Accessed November 20, 2012. http://www.businessweek.com/news/2012-05-14/will-my-baby-die-dna-revelation-comes-too-late.

Lintott CJ, K Schawinski, W Keel, H Van Arkel, N Bennert, E Edmondson, D Thomas, DJB Smith, PD Herbert, MJ Jarvis, S Virani, D Andreescu, SP Bamford, K Land, P Murray, RC Nichol, MJ Raddick, A Slosar, A Szalay, J Vandenberg. "Galaxy Zoo: 'Hanny's Voorwerp', a quasar light echo?" *Monthly notices of the Royal Astronomical Society* 399 no. 1 (2009):129-140. Accessed November 2, 2012. http://onlinelibrary.wiley.com/doi/10.1111/j.1365-2966.2009.15299.x/abstract.

Lisi AG. "An Exceptionally Simple Theory of Everything." *Arxiv.org.* (November 6, 2007): Accessed November 15, 2012.http://arxiv.org/abs/0711.0770.

MacKenzie H. "Peter Thiel: Sometimes the opposite of transparency is criminality." *PandoDaily* April 19, 2012. Accessed November 21, 2012. http://pandodaily.com/2012/04/19/peter-thiel-sometimes-the-opposite-of-transparency-is-criminality/.

Makary M. "How to Stop Hospitals From Killing Us." *Wall Street Journal,* September 21, 2012. Accessed November 20, 2012. http://online.wsj.com/article/SB10000872396390444620104578008263334441352.html.

Mauskop A, BT Altura, RQ Cracco, BM Altura. "Intravenous magnesium sulphate relieves migraine attacks in patients with low serum ionized magnesium levels: a pilot study." *Clin Sci (Lond)* 89 no. 6.(December 1995):633-6.

McFarland M. "Why we care about privacy." Santa Clara University, Markulla Center for Applied Ethics. Accessed November 21, 2012. http://www.scu.edu/ethics/practicing/focusareas/technology/internet/privacy/why-care-about-privacy.html.

McFedries P. "Measuring the impact of altmetrics." IEEE Spectrum. August 2012. Accessed August 19, 2012. http://spectrum.ieee.org/at-work/tech-careers/measuring-the-impact-of-altmetrics.

McGill LS. "The Not-so-fine line between privacy and secrecy." Institute for Ethics & Emerging Technologies. June 30, 2012. Accessed November 14, 2012. http://ieet.org/index.php/IEET/more/6026.

McGraw D. "Hospital Association Fights Digital Data Access for Patients." Center for Democracy and Technology. May 2, 2012. Accessed November 20, 2012. https://www.cdt.org/blogs/deven-mcgraw/0205hospital-association-fights-digital-data-access-patients.

Measured Me. "Should Quantified Self Researchers Protect Themselves with Disclaimers?" Measured Me. October 12, 2012. Accessed November 18, 2012. http://www.measuredme.com/2012/10/should-quantified-self-researchers-protect-themselves-with-disclaimers.html.

Merton T. "After the Night Office—Gethsemani Abbey." *Selected poems of Thomas Merton. Enl Ed. Introduction by Mark Van Doren.* NY: New Directions, ©1944,1967, p. 48-49.

Merz B. "Nobelists take genetics from bench to bedside." *JAMA* 254 no. 22 (December 13,1985):3161.

MMV (Medicines for Malaria Venture): "Open Access Malaria Box." MMV. 2012. Accessed November 15, 2012. http://www.mmv.org/malariabox.

Morris ZS,S Wooding, J Grant. "The answer is 17 years, what is the question: understanding time lags in translational research." *J R Soc Med* 104 (2011): 510–520. DOI 10.1258/jrsm.2011.110180.

National Audubon Society. "American Birds, 2010-2011, the annual summary of the Christmas Bird Count, volume 65." Accessed November 13, 2012. http://birds.audubon.org/american-birds-2010-2011-summary-111th-christmas-bird-count.

National Audubon Society. "Christmas Bird Count." Accessed November 13, 2012. http://birds.audubon.org/christmas-bird-count.

National Audubon Society. "Audubon to Expand Famous Christmas Bird Count.

NIH Clinical Center. "NIH Bedside-to-Bench Program: New! Program Changes Name." 2012. Accessed September 29, 2012. http://clinicalcenter.nih.gov/ccc/btb/.

113th Annual Holiday Count to 'Drop Fees, Add Languages, Go Digital.'" October 23, 2012. Accessed November 13, 2012. http://www.audubon.org/newsroom/press-releases/2012/audubon-expand-famous-christmas-bird-count.

Pariser E. *The filter bubble: what the Internet is hiding from you.* NY: Penguin, ©2011.

Plait P. "Voorwerp! Bad Astronomy." *Discover Magazine.* January 11, 2011, 7:06 AM. Accessed November 13, 2012. http://blogs.discovermagazine.com/badastronomy/2011/01/11/voorwerp/.

Presidential Commission for the Study of Bioethical Issues. *Privacy and Progress in Whole Genome Sequencing.* Accessed November 20, 2012.http://www.bioethics.gov/cms/sites/default/files/PrivacyProgress508.pdf.

Pringsheim T, W Davenport, G Mackie, I Worthington, M Aubé, SN Christie, J Gladstone, WJ Becker; "Canadian Headache Society Prophylactic Guidelines Development Group. Canadian Headache Society guideline for migraine prophylaxis." *Can J Neurol Sci.* 39 no. 2 Suppl 2 (March 2012):S1-59.

Ramadan NM, H Halvorson, A Vande-Linde, SR Levine, JA Helpern, KM Welch. "Low brain magnesium in migraine." *Headache.* 29 no. 7 (July 1989):416-9.

Ramadan NM, H Halvorson, A Vande-Linde, SR Levine, JA Helpern, KM Welch. "Low brain magnesium in migraine." *Headache.* 29 no. 9 (October1989):590-3.

Robbins, Louise S. *Censorship and the American Library: The American Library Association's Response to Threats to Intellectual Freedom, 1939-1969. (Contributions in Librarianship and Information Science, 89)* Westport, CT: Greenwood Press, (c)1996, p.13.

Schwartz O and P Leyden. "The Long Boom: A History of the Future, 1980-2020." *Wired,* July 1997. Accessed November 21, 2012. http://www.wired.com/wired/archive/5.07/long-boom_pr.html.

Solove DJ. "Why privacy matters even if you have 'nothing to hide.'" *Chronicle Review,* May 15, 2011. Accessed November 21, 2012. http://chronicle.com/article/Why-Privacy-Matters-Even-if/127461/.

Spence PR and MC Reddy. "The 'active' gatekeeper in collaborative information seeking activities." *GROUP '07, Proceedings of the 2007 International ACM Conference on Supporting Group Work.* NY: ACM, 2007, 277-280.

Spence PR and MC Reddy. "Beyond Expertise Seeking: A Field Study of the Informal Knowledge Practices of Healthcare IT Teams." *Computer Supported Cooperative Work* 21 no. 2-3 (2012): 283-315.

Swanson DR. "Fish oil, Raynaud's Syndrome, and undiscovered public knowledge." *Perspect Biol Med.* 30 no. 1 (Autumn 1986):7-18.

Swanson DR. "Migraine and magnesium: eleven neglected connections." *Perspect Biol Med.* 31 no. 4 (Summer 1988):526-57.

Swanson DR. "A second example of mutually isolated medical literatures related by implicit, unnoticed connections." *J Am Soc Inf Sci.*40 no. 6 (November 1989):432-5.

Tapscott D. "Why transparency and privacy should go hand in hand." *Huffington Post* July 12, 2010 02:06 PM. Accessed November 21, 2012. http://www.huffingtonpost.com/don-tapscott/why-transparency-and-priv_b_643221.html.

Taleb NN. *The Black Swan: The Impact of the Highly Improbable.* NY: Random House, ©2007.

Taubert K. "Magnesium bei Migrane. Ergebnisse einer multizentrischen Pilotstudie. [Magnesium in migraine. Results of a multicenter pilot study]." *Fortschr Med.* 112 no. 24 (August 30, 1994):328-30.

Tucker S. "The role of data in redefining the relationship between citizen and state." The Young Foundation, November 13, 2012. Accessed November 15, 2012. http://youngfoundation.org/social-innovation-investment/the-role-of-data-in-redefining-the-relationship-between-citizen-and-state/.

US. Department of Health and Human Services (DHHS). "HHS imposes a $4.3 million civil money penalty for violations of the HIPAA Privacy Rule." February 22, 2011. Accessed November 20, 2012.http://www.hhs.gov/news/press/2011pres/02/20110222a.html.

US. House of Representatives. Committee on Homeland Security. "Internet terror recruitment & tradecraft: How can we address an evolving tool while protecting free speech?" Hearing before the Subcommittee on Intelligence, Information Sharing, and Terrorism Risk Assessment of the Committee on Homeland Security, House of Representatives, One Hundred Eleventh Congress, Second Session, May 26, 2010. Serial No. 111–67. Accessed November 20, 2012. http://www.gpo.gov/fdsys/pkg/CHRG-111hhrg63091/html/CHRG-111hhrg63091.htm.

University of Utah, Honors College. *Transparency and privacy, clashing paradigms in a Web 2.0 world. (A University of Utah Honors Think Tank 2012)*. Accessed June 11, 2013. http://www.law.utah.edu/wp-content/uploads/HTT-final-report.pdf.

Van Arkel. "H. 04 | Voorwerp: The Story Behind." Hanny's Voorwerp. November 18, 2008. Accessed November 14, 2012. http://www.hannysvoorwerp.com/?page_id=8.

Wagner CS. *The new invisible college : science for development*. Washington, DC: Brookings Institution Press, ©2008.

Whelan E, R Teigland, B Donnelan, W Golden. "How Internet technologies impact information flows in R&D: reconsidering the technological gatekeeper." *R&D Management* 40 no. 4 (2010):400-413. DOI: 10.1111/j.1467-9310.2010.00610.x

Wilbanks J. "Consent to research."September 18, 2011. Accessed November 20, 2012. http://www.slideshare.net/wilbanks/consent-to-research.

Wilbanks J. "Consent to Research—iDASH webinar."Mar 16, 2012. Accessed November 20, 2012.http://www.slideshare.net/wilbanks/consent-to-research-idash-webinar.

Williamson AE, M Todd, PM Ylioja, J Cronshaw, Z Hungerford. "Open Source Drug Discovery—Malaria (OSDDMalaria)." Accessed November 15, 2012. http://openwetware.org/wiki/Open_Source_Drug_Discovery_-_Malaria.

Zerhouni EA. "Translational and Clinical Science—Time for a New Vision." *New England Journal of Medicine* 353 no. 15 (October 13, 2005):21-1623. DOI: 10.1056/NEJMsb053723. Accessed September 29, 2012. http://www.nejm.org/toc/nejm/353/15/.